FORBIDDEN PLEASURES

New Selected Poems

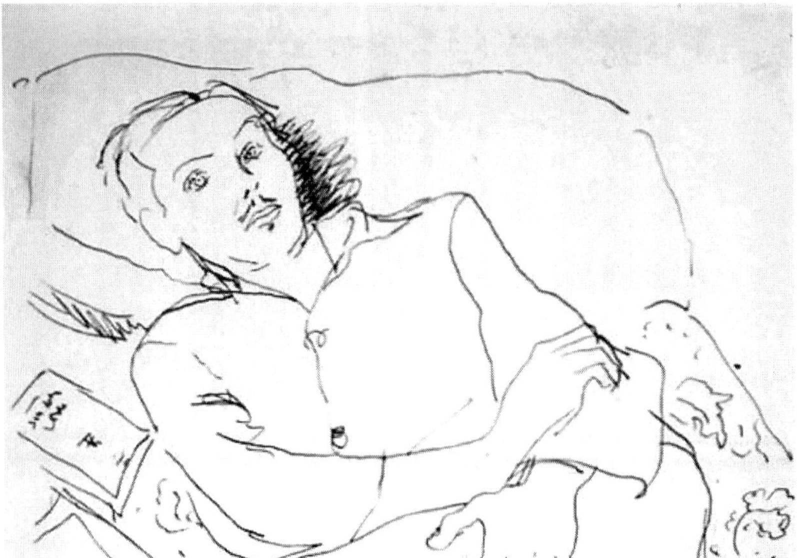

FORBIDDEN PLEASURES

LUIS CERNUDA

NEW SELECTED POEMS

[1924–1949]

Translated by Stephen Kessler

BLACK WIDOW PRESS

Original poems in this book are taken from the second printing of the fourth edition of *La realidad y el deseo*, 1975, Fonda de Culura Económica, México, D. F.

Black Widow Press is an imprint of Commonwealth Books, Inc., Boston, MA. Distributed to the trade by NBN (National Book Network) throughout North America, Canada, and the U.K. All Black Widow Press books are printed on acid-free paper, and glued into bindings. Black Widow Press and its logo are registered trademarks of Commonwealth Books, Inc.

Joseph S. Phillips and Susan J. Wood, Ph.D., Publishers
www.blackwidowpress.com

Cover Photo: Luis Cernuda in Toledo, 1934. Archivo Cernuda, Residencia de Estudiantes, CSIC, Madrid.
Frontispiece: Luis Cernuda. Anonymous sketch, circa 1932. Private collection.
Author Photo: Luis Cernuda in Guadarrama Sierra, near Madrid, 1935. Archivo Cernuda, Residencia de Estudiantes, CSIC, Madrid.

Design, typesetting & production: Kerrie Kemperman

ISBN: 978-09960079-4-8
Printed in the United States

10 9 8 7 6 5 4 3 2 1

Acknowledgments

Some of these translations originally appeared in the following magazines, whose editors are gratefully acknowledged: *Agni, Catamaran Literary Reader, Chicago Quarterly Review, Miramar, New American Writing, Or, Osiris, phren-Z,* and *The Redwood Coast Review.*

The translator also wishes to thank Luis Cernuda's heirs, the Yanguas family of Seville (Ángel Maria Yanguas Cernuda, Ángel Yanguas Álvarez de Toledo, and Ana Yanguas Álvarez de Toledo), for their cooperation and encouragement throughout the course of this project.

Cernuda biographer James Valender in Mexico City has been immensely helpful in his suggestions and enthusiasm. I am grateful to Francisco Segovia for putting us in touch.

Música cautiva, the Cernuda *Antología poética* edited by Fernando Ortiz (Seville, 2002), was of great assistance in my initial selection of poems.

Joe Phillips of Black Widow Press has been instrumental in support of my efforts to bring this book to fruition.

I would also like to express my gratitude to Gavin Andersen and Katie Trostel, who typed the Spanish texts.

Finally, Marc Hofstadter, Rebecca Taksel, Walter Martin, Alta Ifland, Lucas Lackner and Roger Greenwald have made important contributions to sustaining my morale with their critical support and encouragement.

I extend my gratitude to all of the above.

—SK

Contents

LOS PLACERES PROHIBIDOS / FORBIDDEN PLEASURES

DONDE HABITE EL OLVIDO / WHERE OBLIVION LIVES

INVOCACIONES / INVOCATIONS

LAS NUBES / CLOUDS

COMO QUIEN ESPERA EL ALBA / LIKE SOMEONE AWAITING DAWN

VIVIR SIN ESTAR VIVIENDO / TO LIVE WITHOUT BEING ALIVE

Translator's Prologue

A Timeless Contemporary

Writing at the height of Modernism, Luis Cernuda (1902–1963) seems in some respects a throwback to the nineteenth century. His sensibility has more in common with the great European Romantic poets—Hölderlin, Wordsworth, Shelley, Keats, and Bécquer, Cernuda's precursor from Seville—than with such modernist contemporaries as Eliot, Pound, Vallejo, Pessoa, or Valéry. Cavafy is the modern poet with whom he probably has most in common. With a mystical spirituality akin to Hölderlin's, the plainspokenness of Wordsworth, Shelley's neo-Platonism, Keats's worship of Beauty, and Bécquer's impassioned lyricism, Cernuda carries forward their perennial themes and techniques colored by his current historical, social and personal circumstances—war, exile, alienation, homosexuality, heartbreak, nostalgia, existential despair, and the striving for artistic excellence—to compose poems that in the half-century since his death have made him one of the most revered and influential poets in the Spanish-speaking world.

It is only in recent years, mainly through my translations of his prose poems, *Written in Water,* and his later poems, *Desolation of the Chimera,* that this important Spanish poet has become slightly more visible to English-language readers and begun to gain a reputation that properly places him in the company of his more popular peers (and admirers) like García Lorca and the Nobel Prize-winners Pablo Neruda and Octavio Paz. Cernuda occupies a singular place in twentieth-century Spanish-language poetry with his absolutely distinctive if deeply traditional style(s), voice(s), tone(s), and thematic range. Like almost everyone else, he was at first influenced by certain poetic trends of his time, but fairly early in his evolution he turned to cultivate his own unmistakable vocabulary and vision.

While one could hardly say that he "never looked back"—he looked back often, painfully, especially to his lost Spain, with an extremely complex and conflicted mixture of feelings—he pressed ahead with his anomalous project in confidence or faith that, though he felt himself invisible to his contemporaries, his poetry would be discovered and appreciated by subsequent generations. He was wrong to assume he was forgotten in his own time (even during the later years of his exile his poems were being read and admired by Spaniards and Latin Americans) but correct in anticipating future readers. Cernuda is a cosmopolitan poet who, in part because of his marginality and alienation as a political exile, and as a gay man who made no secret of his sexual identity, speaks directly to us in our era of mass displacements and personal migrations, gay pride and gay rights.

Born in Seville, in the heart of Andalucía, where many of his famed peers (Lorca, Pedro Salinas, Rafael Alberti, Vicente Aleixandre) also originated, Cernuda came of age in Madrid in the early thirties in the company of these and such other poets as Jorge Guillén, Gerardo Diego, Dámaso Alonso, and the visiting Chilean Neruda. The "Generation of 1927," one of the most productive creative cohorts of Spanish culture since the Golden Age, in those years of the young Republic embodied an extraordinary surge of artistic activity that radically altered the atmosphere. This rich cultural ferment came to an end, or was at least dispersed, with the onset of the civil war in 1936. At that time Cernuda had just published the first edition of his collected poems, *La realidad y el deseo (Reality and Desire)*, which he would expand and reissue twice under the same title in the remainder of his abbreviated life. He died of a heart attack at sixty-one, in his adopted home of Mexico City, before he had prepared its fourth edition (1964), the third printing of which provides the basis for the present volume.

In a 1935 talk, published as "Words Before a Reading," Cernuda explained the origin of his poetry and his dialectical concept of reality and desire: "The poetic instinct was awakened in me thanks to the most acute perception of reality, when I could feel with the most profound resonance the alluring beauty of the surrounding world. Its effect was, as in a certain way occurs with sexual desire, an urge, painful in its intensity, to abandon myself and to be immersed in that immense body of creation. And what made this desire even more agonizing was the tacit recognition that its fulfillment was impossible." Here we find the seeds of themes that permeate his writings for the rest of his life: an erotic spirituality or mysticism, with its gratifications, revelations, torments, losses, griefs and disappointments. His Andalusian adolescence, with its sexual awakenings on the sunny beaches of the southern coast, remains for Cernuda a paradigm of pure happiness, an archetypal measure of human potential, and finally a lost paradise whose truth only the poet can record.

Like many of his contemporaries, Cernuda started out under the imposing influence of Spain's preceding generation of literary giants, among the most prominent Antonio Machado, Miguel de Unamuno, José Ortega y Gasset, and especially Juan Ramón Jiménez, whose concept of "pure poetry" can be felt strongly in Cernuda's *First Poems* (1927): delicate, formal, exquisitely sensitive songlike lyrics. Not a syllable is wasted in these slim quatrains that register the feelings and sensations of a poet in a critical phase of his formation. With *A River, A Lover* (1929), the young poet ventures into the newly discovered waters of surrealism with its dreamlike logic and slightly more explicit sexuality. The Generation of 1927 adopted the Baroque 300-year-old example of Luis de Góngora as its alternate model of imaginative extravagance in rebellion against the refined poetics of Jiménez, and this shift can be felt most forcefully in Cernuda's fourth book, *Forbidden Pleasures* (1931), where the gay man asserts himself defiantly against the forces of conventional (Catholic) morality and repression, sexual and otherwise. In the opening salvo of that book, "I'll Tell You How You Were Born," Cernuda unleashes the fury of his liberated imagination against anything that would attempt to inhibit the authentic expression of the artist or the passion of the individual.

In his next book, the long poem or series of poems *Where Oblivion Lives* (1933), he turns toward a metaphysical exploration of love, loss and death, bearing down hard on the theme of the inevitable nothingness that follows earthly life, the definitive forgottenness of what's forgotten, and concluding, with the coda "Phantoms of Desire," that the earth itself is the ultimate lover and humans the mere means of transmission for its life force, which is indifferent to our contentment or discontent, let alone happiness.

But it is with *Invocations* (1935) that Cernuda's mature voice begins to emerge in a series of longer poems that prefigure the great odes, meditations, elegies, lyrics and dramatic monologues of his deeper maturity. In poems like "The Lighthouse Keeper's Soliloquy," "The Poet's Glory," "September Wind in the Poplars," "All for Some Yellow Tulips," "Young Man of the Sea," "Hymn to Sadness" and "To the Statues of the Gods" we are given a powerful preview of such later masterpieces as "Full Moon Night," "The Family," "Quetzalcóatl," "Nightingale on a Rock," "To a Future Poet," "The Ruins," and "Night of a Man and His Demon." Throughout his books of the forties—*Clouds* (1940), *Like Someone Awaiting Dawn* (1944), and *To Live without Being Alive* (1949)—there is a seemingly effortless lyricism in the poet's language, a musical yet almost conversational fluency akin to the river (originally the Guadalquivir of his native Seville) that, along with the ocean, he invokes again and again as an image of constancy as well as time and change. Poetry is the only thing that gives at least the illusion of stopping time, of holding an inevitably transient moment of pleasure, of longing, of consciousness, of fulfillment.

Another pervasive theme to be found throughout these books is exile. Even while he is still in Spain, nostalgia informs the poet's apprehension of reality, and once he leaves Spain in 1938—first to teach for ten years in London, Cambridge, and Glasgow (cold gray cities evoked repeatedly in grim terms in these poems), and later at Mount Holyoke College in Massachusetts, before finally moving to Mexico in 1952—his sense of loss and grief at what is happening in Spain during the civil war, and later in the certainty that he can never return to his country, becomes increasingly profound and bitter. This bitterness is in direct proportion to the bliss he remembers or reimagines of his Andalusian youth, and the tension between these polar realities (or reality versus desire) charges his poems with an extraordinary urgency.

Cernuda's mature writings manifest his belief in the poem as a medium of naked truth, neither an intellectual exercise, a career advancer, nor a parlor trick, but a matter of life and death, a deadly serious act of self-realization against both human and cosmic odds, against social ostracism and oblivion itself. His contempt for small-minded critics and bourgeois conformists can be scathing. He never abandons his allegiance to the visionary aristocracy of the artist, the poet especially, even in his darkest moments of despair, stranded in the most inhospitable northern climates. When wandering and exile have come to define his relations with the world and its people, along with the wounds of love and thwarted or fleeting passion, as well as the possibility of never being read or remembered by the readers he had hoped for at the beginning, Cernuda holds nothing back, and his technical mastery enables him to explore the mysteries and agonies of existence with an unabashed passion at times nearly operatic in its intensity. Yet his formal composure is such that he seldom veers into sentimentality, and the poems, for all their rhapsodic sentiment, never abandon critical intelligence. Such nakedness of feeling, even when cloaked in a dramatic persona, can be both disarming and disorienting in an age like the present one, drenched in self-protective irony. Cernuda can be ironic, and darkly funny in a caustic way, but his poems are gravely coherent and they don't play games. My sense is that he is so retro in the current climate as to be radical, so old school as to be avant garde, so traditional in the richest sense that his best poems will prove timeless whenever, and by whomever, they are rediscovered.

My selection for the poems in this volume is based on a personal reading of the poet's work, taking into account Fernando Ortiz's 2002 anthology *Música cautiva (Captive Music)* published in Seville on the occasion of Cernuda's centenary, and also the suggestions of leading Cernuda scholar and biographer James Valender in Mexico City. I have tried to included as many as possible of the poems generally considered Cernuda's best from these years, with the exception of those I felt unable to bring across in English versions that would measure up to the originals. Also of major importance to me has been to convey as richly as possible the full range of the poet's moods, modes, tones, styles, and themes—from lyrical effusions to bitter denunciations, lamentations to celebrations, personal confessions to dramatic projections. Part of Cernuda's genius is his ability to speak in many different voices and personas, and most of them are represented here.

I first found Cernuda in Madrid in 1976 when I picked up a copy of *La realidad y el deseo* in one of the book stalls opposite Atocha Station. On the back of the orange-colored paperback the handsome face of a dapper young man in the bloom of his late twenties (my age at the time) gazed out directly at me, it seemed, with startling immediacy, even though he had been dead for more than a decade. I was seduced—first by this appealing image of the poet and soon by the elegant and intelligible poems within. I tried to translate a few of those poems, even published a few in the late seventies, but I didn't have the experience or the skill required in order to do justice to the originals. After finding a copy of *Ocnos,* his prose poems, in 1999, by then I imagined that I might be able to make them plausible in English. The resulting book was *Written in Water* (City Lights, 2004), and by then I was so immersed in the author and his work that I wanted to go deeper, which resulted in my selection from his last poems (1950–1962), *Desolation of the Chimera* (White Pine Press, 2009). With this book I hope to complement those two and round out the fullest representation in English of this perennially contemporary poet.

The translation of poetry is, for me, a mystery, very much like the strangeness and otherness of original composition. I try to trust my ear and my imagination combined with my knowledge of prosody to find parallels or echoes or equivalents in English for what the poet has written in Spanish. My practice as a translator has evolved from a fairly conservative adherence to the word to a more intuitive reading of meaning, all the while trying to approximate the music and rhythm and feeling of the original with a completely different set of sounds. What may sound roughly "natural" to the Latin ear, to the Anglophone may ring as rhetorical, so the translator may have to lower the temperature of the original a little until it sounds as credible in American as in Castilian. Only the reader can judge the fidelity, the value or success of a translation—*Does it feel true? Does it sound like poetry? Does it speak to me?*—and no translation is definitive, but my goal for these poems in English (compared across the page with the originals) is to give a reliable illusion of what it's like to read them in Cernuda's Spanish.

—Stephen Kessler

from

Primeras Poesías

First Poems

[1924–1927]

I

Va la brisa reciente
Por el espacio esbelta,
Y en las hojas cantando
Abre una primavera.

Sobre el límpido abismo
Del cielo se divisan,
Como dichas primeras,
Primeras golondrinas.

Tan sólo un árbol turba
La distancia que duerme,
Así el fervor alerta
La indolencia presente.

Verdes están las hojas,
El crepúsculo huye,
Anegándose en sombra
Las fugitivas luces.

En su paz la ventana
Restituye a diario
Las estrellas, el aire
Y el que estaba soñando.

I

A fresh breeze blows
Through slender space
And singing in the leaves
A springtime blooms.

Like primal joys,
Primal swallows
Cut clean streaks
Through limpid sky.

A single tree disturbs
The distance fast asleep,
The same way passion stirs
The laziness you feel.

All the leaves are green,
Sunset slips away,
Scattered streaks of light
Drowning in the dark.

The window every day
Peacefully restores
The air, the stars, and one
Who was dreaming there.

XII

Eras, instante, tan claro.
Perdidamente te alejas,
Dejando erguido al deseo
Con su vagas ansias tercas.

Siento huir bajo el otoño
Pálidas aguas sin fuerza,
Mientras se olvidan los árboles
De las hojas que desertan.

La llama tuerce su hastío,
Sola su viva presencia,
Y la lámpara ya duerme
Sobre mis ojos en vela.

Cuán lejano todo. Muertas
Las rosas que ayer abrieran,
Aunque aliente su secreto
Por las verdes alamedas.

Bajo tormentas la playa
Será soledad de arena
Donde el amor yazca en sueños.
La tierra y el mar lo esperan.

XII

Moment, you were so bright,
Now you've slipped away,
Leaving desire proud
Of its persistent ache.

I can feel pale weak waters
In flight under autumn skies,
While all the trees are forgetting
The leaves abandoning them.

The flame twists in disgust,
Alone with its living self,
And while the lamp is sleeping,
My eyes are wide awake.

How far away everything is.
Yesterday's roses are dead,
Although their secret still breathes
Along the green rows of trees.

Under its storms the beach
Is sandy solitude
Where love lies down to dream
Awaited by earth and sea.

XVI

La noche a la ventana.
Ya la luz se ha dormido.
Guardada está la dicha
En el aire vacío.

Levanta entre las hojas,
Tú, mi aurora futura;
No dejes que me anegue
El sueño entre sus plumas.

Pero escapa el deseo
Por la noche entreabierta,
Y en límpido reposo
El cuerpo se contempla.

Acreciente la noche
Sus sombras y su calma,
Que a su rosal la rosa
Volverá la mañana.

Y una vaga promesa
Acunando va el cuerpo.
En vano dichas busca
Por el aire el deseo.

XVI

Night at the dark window.
Light has gone to sleep.
Happiness is sheltered
Under the empty sky.

You, my future dawn,
Are rising between the leaves;
Don't let my dream be drowned
Up there among their plumes.

And yet desire escapes
Into what's left of night,
And in that clear repose
The body regards itself.

Night extends its shadows,
Its darkness and its calm,
So that in the morning
The rose returns to its bush.

The body goes on rocking
Some promise in its cradle.
Desire searches in vain
For happiness in the air.

XVIII

Los muros nada más.
Yace la vida inerte,
Sin vida, sin ruido,
Sin palabras crueles.

La luz lívida escapa
Y el cristal ya se afirma
Contra la noche incierta,
De arrebatadas lluvias.

Alzada resucita
Tal otra vez la casa;
Los tiempos son idénticos,
Distintas las miradas.

¿He cerrado la puerta?
El olvido me abre
Sus desnudas estancias
Grises, blancas, sin aire.

Pero nadie suspira.
Un llanto entre las manos
Sólo. Silencio; nada.
La oscuridad temblando.

XVIII

The walls and nothing else.
Life lies here inert,
Lifeless, without a sound,
Without any cruel words.

Purple light escapes
And the window asserts itself
Against the uncertain night
Of thrashing, driving rain.

The house is stirred from sleep
Again, just as before;
The times are just the same,
Only the gazes different.

Did I lock the door?
Oblivion opens in me
All its empty shelves,
Airless, gray and blank.

And yet nobody breathes.
Only a single cry
Into my hands. Silence;
Nothing. Darkness trembling.

XXIII

Escondido en los muros
Este jardín me brinda
Sus ramas y sus aguas
De secreta delicia.

Qué silencio. ¿Es así
El mundo? Cruza el cielo
Desfilando paisajes,
Risueño hacia lo lejos.

Tierra indolente. En vano
Resplandece el destino.
Junto a las aguas quietas
Sueño y pienso que vivo.

Mas el tiempo ya tasa
El poder de esta hora;
Madura su medida
Escapa entre sus rosas.

Y el aire fresco vuelve
Con la noche cercana,
Su tersura olvidando
Las ramas y las aguas.

XXIII

Hidden inside these walls
The garden lifts its branches
And toasts me with its waters
Spilling secret pleasure.

What silence. Is this what the world
Is like? Streaks of happiness
Across distant skies
Align the landscapes below.

Indolent land. Destiny
Shines its light in vain.
Beside these quiet waters
I dream and believe I'm alive.

But time is closing down
The power of this moment;
Ripening, its measure
Escapes into its roses.

And cool air returns
With the falling night,
The branches and the fountains
Forgetting their perfection.

from

Un Río, Un Amor

A River, A Lover

[1929]

REMORDIMIENTO EN TRAJE DE NOCHE

Un hombre gris avanza por la calle de niebla;
No lo sospecha nadie. Es un cuerpo vacío;
Vacío como pampa, como mar, como viento,
Desiertos tan amargos bajo un cielo implacable.

Es el tiempo pasado, y sus alas ahora
Entre la sombra encuentran una pálida fuerza;
Es el remordimiento, que de noche, dudando,
En secreto aproxima su sombra descuidada.

No estrechéis esa mano. La yedra altivamente
Ascenderá cubriendo los troncos del invierno.
Invisible en la calma el hombre gris camina.
¿No sentís a los muertos? Mas la tierra está sorda.

Remorse Dressed as Night

A gray man is coming down the foggy street;
No one suspects him. He's an empty body;
Empty as the plain, the ocean, wind,
Such bitter deserts under ruthless skies.

He is time gone by, and now its wings
Encounter some faded force in the dark;
It is remorse, which at night, unsure of itself,
Secretly approaches its reckless shadow.

Don't take that hand. Ivy will climb
And choke the trunks of winter in its grip.
Unseen in the calm the gray man walks on.
Can't you feel the dead? But the earth is deaf.

QUISIERA ESTAR SOLO EN EL SUR

Quizá mis lentos ojos no verán más el sur
De ligeros paisajes dormidos en el aire,
Con cuerpos a la sombra de ramas como flores
O huyendo en un galope de caballos furiosos.

El sur es un desierto que llora mientras canta,
Y esa voz no se extingue como pájaro muerto;
Hacia el mar encamina sus deseos amargos
Abriendo un eco débil que vive lentamente.

En el sur tan distante quiero estar confundido.
La lluvia allí no es más que una rosa entreabierta;
Su niebla misma ríe, risa blanca en el viento.
Su oscuridad, su luz son bellezas iguales.

I'd Like to Be Alone in the South

Perhaps my lazy eyes won't see the south again
With its light landscapes drowsing in the air,
Its flowerlike bodies lying in the shade
Or running away at a gallop like mad horses.

The south is a desert crying as it sings,
And that voice never stops like a dead bird;
It sends its bitter desire down to the sea
Creating a faint echo that takes its time.

I want to be blended with that distant south,
The rain there is nothing but an opening rose;
Its very fog laughs, a white laugh in the wind.
Its darkness and its light are equally lovely.

SOMBRAS BLANCAS

Sombras frágiles, blancas, dormidas en la playa,
Dormidas en su amor, en su flor de universo,
El ardiente color de la vida ignorando
Sobre un lecho de arena y de azar abolido.

Libremente los besos desde sus labios caen
En el mar indomable como perlas inútiles;
Perlas grises o acaso cenicientas estrellas
Ascendiendo hacia el cielo con luz desvanecida.

Bajo la noche el mundo silencioso naufraga;
Bajo la noche rostros fijos, muertos, se pierden.
Sólo esas sombras blancas, oh blancas, sí, tan blancas.
La luz también da sombras, pero sombras azules.

White Shadows

Fragile white shadows, sleeping on the beach,
Asleep in their love, in their flowerlike universe,
Knowing nothing of life's blazing colors
On a bed of sand and chance that's been abolished.

Freely the kisses fall from their lips
Into the untamed sea like useless pearls;
Gray pearls or possibly burnt out stars
Rising into the sky scattering light.

In the dark of night the silent world is shipwrecked;
In the dark of night known faces, dead, are lost.
Those white shadows alone, those white, white shadows.
Light also casts its shadows, but they're blue.

DESTIERRO

Ante las puertas bien cerradas,
Sobre un río de olvido, va la canción antigua.
Una luz lejos piensa
Como a través de un cielo.
Todos acaso duermen,
Mientras él lleva su destino a solas.

Fatiga de estar vivo, de estar muerto,
Con frío en vez de sangre,
Con frío que sonríe insinuando
Por las aceras apagadas.

Le abandona la noche y la aurora lo encuentra,
Tras sus huellas la sombra tenazmente.

Exile

Facing the locked doors
Above a river of oblivion,
As the old song says.
One distant light is thinking
On the far side of the sky.
Maybe everyone else is sleeping
While he shoulders his destiny, alone.

Tired of being alive, of being dead,
Blood in his veins gone cold,
The cold flashing a subtle smile
Along darkened sidewalks.

Night leaves him and dawn meets him,
Darkness following stubbornly in his tracks.

NEVADA

En el estado de Nevada
Los caminos de hierro tienen nombres de pájaro,
Son de nieve los campos
Y de nieve las horas.

Las noches transparentes
Abren luces soñadas
Sobre las aguas o tejados puros
Constelados de fiesta.

Las lágrimas sonríen,
La tristeza es de alas,
Y las alas, sabemos,
Dan amor inconstante.

Los árboles abrazan árboles,
Una canción besa otra canción;
Por los caminos de hierro
Pasa el dolor y la alegría.

Siempre hay nieve dormida
Sobre otra nieve, allá en Nevada.

Nevada

In the State of Nevada
The iron roads are named for birds,
Snow blankets the landscape
And time is measured in snow.

The clear nights
Open dreamy lights
Over the waters or the clean rooftops
Lit up for the festivities.

Tears laugh,
Sadness has wings,
And wings, as we know,
Are faithless in love.

Trees embrace trees,
One song kisses another;
Down the iron roads
Go pain and joy.

There's always snow asleep
On other snow, out there in Nevada.

COMO EL VIENTO

Como el viento a lo largo de la noche,
Amor en pena o cuerpo solitario,
Toca en vano a los vidrios,
Sollozando abandona las esquinas;

O como a veces marcha en la tormenta,
Gritando locamente,
Con angustia de insomnio,
Mientras gira la lluvia delicada;

Sí, como el viento al que un alba le revela
Su tristeza errabunda por la tierra,
Su tristeza sin llanto,
Su fuga sin objeto;

Como él mismo extranjero,
Como el viento huyo lejos.
Y sin embargo vine como luz.

Like the Wind

Like the wind blowing all night long,
Tapping in vain at the windows,
A solitary body or grieving lover
Wanders the streets sobbing;

Or sometimes goes out walking in a storm
Screaming like a madman
Unable to sleep in his anguish
While the rain swirls lightly about;

Yes, like the wind whose sadness dawn reveals
To be wandering over the earth,
Its sadness without a cry,
Its aimless flight;

Like the wind itself a stranger,
Like the wind I try to escape,
And still I came like light.

ESTOY CANSADO

Estar cansado tiene plumas,
Tiene plumas graciosas como un loro,
Plumas que desde luego nunca vuelan,
Mas balbucean igual que loro.

Estoy cansado de las casas,
Prontamente en ruinas sin un gesto;
Estoy cansado de las cosas,
Con un latir de seda vueltas luego de espaldas.

Estoy cansado de estar vivo,
Aunque más cansado sería el estar muerto;
Estoy cansado del estar cansado
Entre plumas ligeras sagazmente,
Plumas del loro aquel tan familiar o triste,
El loro aquel del siempre estar cansado.

I'm Tired

Being tired has feathers,
Lovely feathers like a parrot's,
Feathers that haven't flown for a long time,
Yet they babble just like a parrot.

I'm tired of houses
Suddenly turned to ruins just like that;
I'm tired of things
Turning their backs with a rustling of silk.

I'm tired of being alive,
Though being dead would be even more tiring;
I'm tired of being tired
So wisely among light feathers,
Feathers of that sad parrot I know so well,
That parrot who always sounds so tired.

EL CASO DEL PÁJARO ASESINADO

Nunca sabremos, nunca,
Por qué razón un día
Esas luces temblaron levemente;
Fue una llorosa espuma,
Una brisa más grande, nada acaso.
Sólo las olas saben.

Por eso hoy muestran desdeñosas
Su color de miradas,
Su color ignorante todavía, aunque un recuerdo
Les cante algo, algo levemente.

Fue un pájaro quizá asesinado;
Nadie sabe. Por nadie
O por alguien quizá triste en las piedras,
En los muros del cielo.

Mas de ello hoy nada se sabe.
Sólo un temblor de luces levemente,
Un color de miradas en las olas o en la brisa;
También, acaso, un miedo.
Todo, es verdad, inseguro.

The Case of the Murdered Bird

Never, we'll never know
Why it was that one day
Those lights flickered a little;
It was some tears of spray,
A gust of wind, maybe nothing.
Only the waves could say.

That's why today their color
Looks like it doesn't care,
Still in the dark, though a memory
Faintly sings them a song.

Perhaps a bird was murdered;
Nobody knows. By no one
Or by someone sad
In the stone walls of the sky.

But nothing is known of that.
Just some flickering lights,
The color of a look in the waves or the wind;
Maybe a fear as well.
True, nobody can be sure.

DESDICHA

Un día comprendió cómo sus brazos eran
Solamente de nubes;
Imposible con nubes estrechar hasta el fondo
Un cuerpo, una fortuna.

La fortuna es redonda y cuenta lentamente
Estrellas del estío.
Hacen falta unos brazos seguros como el viento,
Y como el mar un beso.

Pero él con sus labios,
Con sus labios no sabe sino decir palabras;
Palabras hacia el techo,
Palabras hacia el suelo,
Y sus brazos son nubes que transforman la vida
En aire navegable.

Bad Luck

One day he knew his arms
Were made merely of clouds;
With clouds it was impossible to hold
A body, a fortune.

Fortune is round and slowly counts
Stars in the summer night.
All that's missing is arms strong as the wind,
And like the ocean, a kiss.

But he has just his lips,
His lips that speak only words;
Words said to the ceiling,
Words dropped to the floor,
And his arms are clouds that turn all life
Into a navigable sky.

NO INTENTEMOS EL AMOR NUNCA

Aquella noche el mar no tuvo sueño.
Cansado de contar, siempre contar a tantas olas,
Quiso vivir hacia lo lejos,
Donde supiera alguien de su color amargo.

Con una voz insomne decía cosas vagas,
Barcos entrelazados dulcemente
En un fondo de noche,
O cuerpos siempre pálidos, con su traje de olvido
Viajando hacia nada.

Cantaba tempestades, estruendos desbocados
Bajo cielos con sombra,
Como la sombra misma,
Como la sombra siempre
Rencorosa de pájaros estrellas.

Su voz atravesando luces, lluvia, frío,
Alcanzaba ciudades elevadas a nubes,
Cielo Sereno, Colorado, Glaciar del Infierno,
Todas puras de nieve o de astros caídos
En sus manos de tierra.

Mas el mar se cansaba de esperar las ciudades.
Allí su amor tan sólo era un pretexto vago
Con sonrisa de antaño,
Ignorado de todos.

Y con sueño de nuevo se volvió lentamente
Adonde nadie
Sabe nada de nadie.
Adonde acaba el mundo.

Let's Never Try to Make Love

That night the ocean couldn't sleep.
Tired of counting, always counting all those waves,
It wanted to live somewhere far away,
Where someone might understand its bitter color.

With a sleepless voice it told vague stories
Of boats tenderly entwined
Against a night sky background,
Or endlessly pale bodies dressed in forgetting
Traveling toward nothing.

It sang storms, thunderclaps unleashed
Under shadowy skies,
Like darkness itself,
Like the always angry
Darkness of starlike birds.

Its voice crossing lights, rain, cold,
Reached cities lifted into clouds,
Serene Sky, Pink Place, Hell's Glacier,
All made purely of snow or of stars
Fallen into earthly hands.

But the ocean grew tired of waiting for the cities.
There its love was merely an empty pretext
With an outdated smile
Nobody recognized.

And sleepy once more, slowly it turned
Back to where no one
Knows anything of anyone.
Where the world comes to an end.

RAZÓN DE LAS LÁGRIMAS

La noche por ser triste carece de fronteras.
Su sombra, en rebelión como la espuma,
Rompe los muros débiles
Avergonzados de blancura;
Noche que no puede ser otra cosa sino noche.

Acaso los amantes acuchillan estrellas,
Acaso la aventura apague una tristeza.
Mas tú, noche, impulsada por deseos
Hasta la palidez del agua,
Aguardas siempre en pie quién sabe a cuáles ruiseñores.

Más allá se estremecen los abismos
Poblados de serpientes entre pluma,
Cabecera de enfermos
No mirando otra cosa que la noche
Mientras cierran el aire entre los labios.

La noche, la noche deslumbrante,
Que junto a las esquinas retuerce sus caderas,
Aguardando, quien sabe,
Como yo, como todos.

Tears' Reasons

Night in its sadness knows no bounds.
Its darkness, in rebellion like the foam,
Breaks weak walls
Ashamed of being white;
Night that can't be anything but night.

Lovers may sometimes stab out holes for stars,
Adventure may at times eclipse a sadness.
But you, night, driven by desires
Thirsty for pale water, stand
Watch always for who knows what nightingales.

Out there great voids spread
Crowded with snakes and feathers,
At the head of a sickbed
Looking out at nothing but the night,
Holding their breath.

Night, brilliant night,
Tilting its hips just so on street corners,
Waiting, who knows,
Like me, like everyone.

DEJADME SOLO

Una verdad es color de ceniza,
Otra verdad es color de planeta;
Mas todas las verdades, desde el suelo hasta el suelo,
No valen la verdad sin color de verdades,
La verdad ignorante de cómo el hombre suele encarnarse en la
nieve.

En cuanto a la mentira, basta decirle "quiero"
Para que brote entre las piedras
Su flor, que en vez de hojas luce besos,
Espinas en lugar de espinas.

La verdad, la mentira,
Como labios azules,
Una dice, otra dice;
Pero nunca pronuncian verdades o mentiras su secreto torcido;
Verdades o mentiras
Son pájaros que emigran cuando los ojos mueren.

Leave Me Alone

One truth is the color of ashes,
Another is the color of the planet,
But all truths, from one ground to another,
Are not worth the truth without truth's colors,
The ignorant truth of how a man can take the form of snow.

As for lies, it's enough to say "I love"
For their flower to spring from between
The rocks, and instead of leaves they shine with kisses,
And instead of thorns, thorns.

Truth, lies,
Like blue lips,
Say one thing and then the other;
But neither truths nor lies ever tell their twisted secret;
Truths or lies
Are birds that migrate when the eyes die.

VIEJA RIBERA

Tanto ha llovido desde entonces,
Entonces, cuando los dientes no eran carne, sino días
Pequeños como un río ignorante
A sus padres llamando porque siente sueño,
Tanto ha llovido desde entonces,
Que ya el paso se olvida en la cabeza.

Unos dicen que sí, otros dicen que no;
Mas sí y no son dos alas pequeñas,
Equilibrio de un cielo dentro de otro cielo,
Como un amor está dentro de otro,
Como el olvido está dentro del olvido.

Si el suplicio con ira pide fiestas
Entre las noches más viriles,
No haremos otra cosa que apuñalar la vida,
Sonreír ciegamente a la derrota,
Mientras los años, muertos como un muerto,
Abren su tumba de estrellas apagadas.

Old Riverbank

It's rained so much since then,
Then, when teeth weren't flesh, but little
Days like a river that doesn't hear
Its parents calling because it's drowsy,
It's rained so much since then
That now your head can't remember the way.

Some say yes, others no;
But yes and no are just two tiny wings,
One sky balancing inside another,
The way one love is inside another,
The way forgetting is inside forgetting.

If your punishment angrily calls for celebrations
In the most virile nights,
We have no choice but to plunge our knife
Into life, blindly grinning at its defeat,
While the years, dead as a dead man,
Open their grave of burnt out stars.

LA CANCIÓN DEL OESTE

Jinete sin cabeza,
Jinete como un niño buscando entre rastrojos
Llaves recién cortadas,
Víboras seductoras, desastres suntuosos,
Navíos para tierra lentamente de carne,
De carne hasta morir igual que muere un hombre.

A lo lejos
Una hoguera transforma en ceniza recuerdos,
Noches como una sola estrella,
Sangre extraviada por las venas un día,
Furia color de amor,
Amor color de olvido,
Aptos ya solamente para triste buhardilla.

Lejos canta el oeste,
Aquel oeste que las manos antaño
Creyeron apresar como el aire a la luna;
Mas la luna es madera, las manos se liquidan
Gota a gota, idénticas a lágrimas.

Olvidemos pues todo, incluso al mismo oeste;
Olvidemos que un día las miradas de ahora
Lucirán a la noche, como tantos amantes,
Sobre el lejano oeste,
Sobre amor más lejano.

Song of the West

Headless horseman,
Childlike rider searching amid the stubble
For recently cut keys,
Seductive snakes, sumptuous disasters,
Ships run aground slowly turning to flesh,
To flesh so they can die the same as men.

In the distance
A bonfire turns memories to ashes,
Nights like a single star,
Blood gone missing from its veins one day,
Fury the color of love,
Love the color of oblivion,
Fit now only for some sad garret.

In the distance the West is singing,
That same West yesterday's hands
Believed they could capture the way air catches the moon;
But the moon is wooden, and hands are liquidated
Drop by drop, exactly like tears.

So let's forget it all, the West included;
Let's forget that someday today's gazes
Will shine at night, like so many lovers,
Over the distant West,
Over the farthest love.

COMO LA PIEL

Ventana huérfana con cabellos habituales,
Gritos del viento,
Atroz paisaje entre cristal de roca,
Prostituyendo los espejos vivos,
Flores clamando a gritos
Su inocencia anterior a obesidades.

Esas cuevas de luces venenosas
Destrozan los deseos, los durmientes;
Luces como lenguas hendidas
Penetrando en los huesos hasta hallar la carne,
Sin saber que en el fondo no hay fondo,
No hay nada, sino un grito,
Un grito, otro deseo
Sobre una trampa de adormideras crueles.

En un mundo de alambre
Donde el olvido vuela por debajo del suelo,
En un mundo de angustia,
Alcohol amarillento,
Plumas de fiebre,
Ira subiendo a un cielo de vergüenza,
Algún día nuevamente resurgirá la flecha
Que abandona el azar
Cuando una estrella muere como otoño para olvidar su sombra.

Like Skin

Orphaned window with the usual long hair,
Shrieking wind,
Horrible landscape of rocky shards,
Turning living mirrors into whores,
Flowers protesting
Their innocence before the obesities.

Those caves of poisonous light
Destroy desires, sleepers;
Lights like split tongues
Piercing through bones down to the flesh,
Not knowing that at bottom there's no bottom,
There's nothing, just a cry,
A cry, another desire
Over a trap door of ruthless poppies.

In a world made of wire
Where oblivion flies underground,
In a world of suffering,
Yellowish alcohol,
Feathery fevers,
Rage climbing into a sky of shame,
Someday the arrow of abandoned chance
Will fly again
When a star goes out like fall to forget its shadow.

from

Los Placeres Prohibidos

Forbidden Pleasures

[1931]

DIRÉ CÓMO NACISTEIS

Diré cómo nacisteis, placeres prohibidos,
Como nace un deseo sobre torres de espanto,
Amenazadores barrotes, hiel descolorida,
Noche petrificada a fuerza de puños,
Ante todos, incluso el más rebelde,
Apto solamente en la vida sin muros.

Corazas infranqueables, lanzas o puñales,
Todo es bueno si deforma un cuerpo;
Tu deseo es beber esas hojas lascivas
O dormir en esa agua acariciadora.
No importa;
Ya declaran tu espíritu impuro.

No importa la pureza, los dones que un destino
Levantó hacia las aves con manos imperecederas;
No importa la juventud, sueño más que hombre,
La sonrisa tan noble, playa de seda bajo la tempestad
De un régimen caído.

Placeres prohibidos, planetas terrenales,
Miembros de mármol con sabor de estío,
Jugo de esponjas abandonadas por el mar,
Flores de hierro, resonantes como el pecho de un hombre.

Soledades altivas, coronas derribadas,
Libertades memorables, manto de juventudes;
Quien insulta esos frutos, tinieblas en la lengua,
Es vil como un rey, como sombra de rey
Arrastrándose a los pies de la tierra
Para conseguir un trozo de vida.

I'll Tell You How You Were Born

I'll tell you how you were born, forbidden pleasures,
The way a desire is born on towers of terror,
Menacing bars, tainted bile,
Night petrified by pummeling fists,
You above all, including the most rebellious,
Fit only for a life beyond all walls.

Bulletproof armor, lances, daggers—
Whatever deforms a body is just fine;
Your desire is to drink from those lascivious leaves
Or lie down to sleep in those caressing waters.
It doesn't matter;
Already your spirit has been stamped impure.

Purity doesn't matter, the gifts that destiny
Flung up toward the birds with deathless hands;
Youth doesn't matter, more dream than flesh and blood,
Such a noble smile, a silken beach raked by the storm
Of a fallen regime.

Forbidden pleasures, earthly planets,
Marble limbs tasting of summer,
Juice from sponges the ocean abandoned,
Iron flowers, echoing like a human chest.

Proud solitudes, overthrown crowns,
Unforgettable freedoms, the mantle of youth;
Whoever insults those fruits, their mouth full of darkness,
Is as vile as a king, the shadow of a king
Dragging itself across the filthy ground
Scrounging for a piece of real life.

No sabía los límites impuestos,
Límites de metal o papel,
Ya que el azar le hizo abrir los ojos bajo una luz tan alta,
Adonde no llegan realidades vacías,
Leyes hediondas, códigos, ratas de paisajes derruídos.

Extender entonces la mano
Es hallar una montaña que prohibe,
Un bosque impenetrable que niega,
Un mar que traga adolescentes rebeldes.

Pero si la ira, el ultraje, el oprobio y la muerte,
Ávidos dientes sin carne todavía,
Amenazan abriendo sus torrentes,
De otro lado vosotros, placeres prohibidos,
Bronce de orgullo, blasfemia que nada precipita,
Tendéis en una mano el misterio,
Sabor que ninguna amargura corrompe,
Cielos, cielos relampagueantes que aniquilan.

Abajo, estatuas anónimas,
Sombras de sombras, miseria, preceptos de niebla;
Una chispa de aquellos placeres
Brilla en la hora vengativa.
Su fulgor puede destruir vuestro mundo.

I never understood the limits that were set,
Metal limits, paper limits,
Since chance tore open my eyes under a light so high
That empty realities can never reach,
Codes of conduct, putrid laws, rats in ruined landscapes.

To reach out your hand in such a place
Is to find a mountain of prohibitions,
An impenetrable forest of negations,
An ocean that swallows rebellious adolescents.

Yet if anger, outrage, rebuke and death,
Ravenous teeth still hungry for flesh,
Threaten to unleash their floodwaters,
From the other side you, forbidden pleasures,
Bronze pride, irrepressible blasphemy,
Open your hands full of mystery,
A taste no bitterness can ever spoil,
Skies, skies full of annihilating lightning.

Down below, nameless statues,
Shadows of shadows, misery, foggy commandments;
One spark of those pleasures
Flashing its revenge—
Its brilliance can obliterate your world.

QUÉ RUIDO TAN TRISTE

Qué ruido tan triste el que hacen dos cuerpos cuando se aman,
Parece como el viento que se mece en otoño
Sobre adolescentes mutilados,
Mientras las manos llueven,
Manos ligeras, manos egoístas, manos obscenas,
Cataratas de manos que fueron un día
Flores en el jardín de un diminuto bolsillo.

Las flores son arena y los niños son hojas,
Y su leve ruido es amable al oído
Cuando ríen, cuando aman, cuando besan,
Cuando besan al fondo
De un hombre joven y cansado
Porque antaño soñó mucho día y noche.

Mas los niños no saben,
Ni tampoco las manos llueven como dicen;
Así el hombre, cansado de estar solo con sus sueños,
Invoca los bolsillos que abandonan arena,
Arena de las flores,
Para que un día decoren su semblante de muerto.

What a Sad Sound

What a sad sound, two bodies making love,
It sounds like the autumn wind moving around
Above mutilated adolescents,
While hands pour down like rain,
Light hands, vain hands, obscene hands,
Torrents of hands that once were flowers
In a garden inside some tiny pocket.

Flowers are sand and boys are leaves,
And their light rustling is kind to the ear
When they laugh, when they love, when they kiss,
When they kiss the soul
Of a tired young man
Because he once dreamed so much, both night and day.

But boys don't know,
Not even hands pour down the way they say;
And so a man, tired of dreaming all alone,
Invokes the little pockets spilling sand,
The sand of flowers,
So that his corpse may one day wear them like a crown.

NO DECÍA PALABRAS

No decía palabras,
Acercaba tan sólo un cuerpo interrogante,
Porque ignoraba que el deseo es una pregunta
Cuya respuesta no existe,
Una hoja cuya rama no existe,
Un mundo cuyo cielo no existe.

La angustia se abre paso entre los huesos,
Remonta por las venas
Hasta abrirse en la piel,
Surtidores de sueño
Hechos carne en interrogación vuelta a las nubes.

Un roce al paso,
Una mirada fugaz entre las sombras,
Bastan para que el cuerpo se abra en dos,
Ávido de recibir en sí mismo
Otro cuerpo que sueñe;
Mitad y mitad, sueño y sueño, carne y carne,
Iguales en figura, iguales en amor, iguales en deseo.

Aunque sólo sea una esperanza,
Porque el deseo es una pregunta cuya respuesta nadie sabe.

He Didn't Say a Word

He didn't say a word,
A questioning body just kept coming closer,
Because it didn't know desire is a question
Whose answer does not exist,
A leaf whose branch does not exist,
A world whose heaven does not exist.

Anguish opens its pathway through the bones,
It climbs through the veins
To bloom in the skin,
Spurts of dreams
Made flesh in their questionings turned into clouds.

A passing touch,
A fleeting glance in the shadows
Are enough to split a body in two,
Eager to receive into itself
Another dreaming body;
Half and half, dream and dream, flesh and flesh,
Equal in form, equal in love, equal in desire.

Even if it's nothing more than a hope,
Because desire is a question whose answer no one knows.

ESTABA TENDIDO

Estaba tendido y tenía entre mis brazos un cuerpo como seda. Lo besé en los labios, porque el río pasaba por debajo. Entonces se burló de mi amor.

Sus espaldas parecían dos alas plegadas. Lo besé en las espaldas, porque el agua sonaba debajo de nosotros. Entonces lloró al sentir la quemadura de mis labios.

Era un cuerpo tan maravilloso que se desvaneció entre mis brazos. Besé su huella; mis lágrimas la borraron. Como el agua continuaba fluyendo, dejé caer en ella un puñal, un ala y una sombra.

De mi mismo cuerpo recorté otra sombra, que sólo me sigue a la mañana. Del puñal y el ala, nada sé.

I Was Lying Down

I was lying down, and in my arms I was holding a silken body. I kissed its lips because the river was flowing below us. Then it made fun of my love.

Its shoulderblades looked like folded wings. I kissed its back, because you could hear the water running beneath us. Then it started crying, burned by the touch of my lips.

It was such a beautiful body it dissolved in my embrace. I kissed the trace it left; my tears washed it away. Since the water was still flowing, I dropped a dagger, a wing and a shadow into it.

Then I cut a shadow off my own body, and it follows me every morning. What happened to the dagger and the wing, I have no idea.

SI EL HOMBRE PUDIERA DECIR

Si el hombre pudiera decir lo que ama,
Si el hombre pudiera levantar su amor por el cielo
Como una nube en la luz;
Si como muros que se derrumban,
Para saludar la verdad erguida en medio,
Pudiera derrumbar su cuerpo, dejando sólo la verdad de su amor,
La verdad de sí mismo,
Que no se llama gloria, fortuna o ambición,
Sino amor o deseo,
Yo sería aquel que imaginaba;
Aquel que con su lengua, sus ojos y sus manos
Proclama ante los hombres la verdad ignorada,
La verdad de su amor verdadero.

Libertad no conozco sino la libertad de estar preso en alguien
Cuyo nombre no puedo oír sin escalofrío;
Alguien por quien me olvido de esta existencia mezquina,
Por quien el día y la noche son para mí lo que quiera,
Y mi cuerpo y espíritu flotan en su cuerpo y espíritu
Como leños perdidos que el mar anega o levanta
Libremente, con la libertad del amor,
La única libertad que me exalta,
La única libertad porque muero.

Tú justificas mi existencia:
Si no te conozco, no he vivido;
Si muero sin conocerte, no muero, porque no he vivido.

If Only a Man Could Say

If only a man could say what he loves,
If only a man could lift his love into the air
Like a cloud in daylight;
If only like walls coming down
To salute the truth that's standing between them,
He could come down around his own body, leaving just the truth
of his love,
The truth of himself,
Which is not called glory, fortune or ambition,
But love or desire,
I would be that man I imagined;
The one with his tongue, his eyes and his hands
Proclaiming in front of everyone the unknown truth,
The truth of his true love.

I know no freedom but that of the imprisoned
In someone whose name I can't hear without a shudder;
Someone who makes me forget this petty life,
Forget the difference between day and night,
And my body and spirit are carried on his
Like logs adrift on the ocean sinking or floating
Freely, with the freedom of love,
The only freedom that exalts me,
The only freedom I'll die for.

You justify my existence:
Not knowing you, I've never lived;
If I die not knowing you, I'll never die, because I haven't lived.

UNOS CUERPOS SON COMO FLORES

Unos cuerpos son como flores,
Otros como puñales,
Otros como cintas de agua;
Pero todos, temprano o tarde,
Serán quemaduras que en otro cuerpo se agranden,
Convirtiendo por virtud del fuego a una piedra en un hombre.

Pero el hombre se agita en todas direcciones,
Sueña con libertades, compite con el viento,
Hasta que un día la quemadura se borra,
Volviendo a ser piedra en el camino de nadie.

Yo, que no soy piedra, sino camino
Que cruzan al pasar los pies desnudos,
Muero de amor por todos ellos;
Les doy mi cuerpo para que lo pisen,
Aunque les lleve a una ambición o a una nube,
Sin que ninguno comprenda
Que ambiciones o nubes
No valen un amor que se entrega.

Some Bodies Are Like Flowers

Some bodies are like flowers,
Others like daggers,
Others like ribbons of water;
But all of them, sooner or later,
Will be wildfires feeding on another body
Turned by fire into a stone in a man.

But a man gets shaken in all directions,
He dreams of freedoms, competes with the wind,
Until one day the blaze consumes him,
Turning him back into a stone in no one's road.

I, who am not a stone but a road
Walked on by naked feet,
Am dying of love for them all;
I give them my body to walk on,
Even though they're bound for an ambition or a cloud,
Not one of them understanding
That neither clouds nor ambitions
Will ever be worth one wholly surrendered love.

ESPERABA SOLO

Esperaba algo, no sabía qué. Esperaba al anochecer, los sábados. Unos me daban limosna, otros me miraban, otros pasaban de largo sin verme.

Tenía en la mano una flor; no recuerdo qué flor era. Pasó un adolescente que, sin mirar, la rozó con su sombra. Yo tenía la mano tendida.

Al caer, la flor se convirtió en un monte. Detrás se ponía un sol; no recuerdo si era negro.

Mi mano quedó vacía. En su palma apareció una gota de sangre.

I Waited All Alone

I was waiting for something, I didn't know what. I waited as the sun was going down, on Saturdays. Some people gave me a few coins, others looked at me, others passed by without seeing me.

I was holding a flower in my hand; I don't recall what kind. An adolescent boy went by, not even looking; his shadow grazed it. I held out my hand.

The flower fell and turned into a mountain. A sun went down behind it; I don't remember whether it was black.

Then my hand was empty. A drop of blood appeared in its palm.

DÉJAME ESTA VOZ

Déjame esta voz que tengo,
Lo mismo que a la pampa le dejan
Sus matorrales de deseo,
Sus ríos secos colgando de las piedras.

Déjame vivir como acero mohoso
Sin puño, tirado en las nubes;
No quiero saber de la gloria envidiosa
Con rabo y cuernos de ceniza.

Un anillo tuve de luna
Tendida en la noche a comienzos de otoño;
Lo di a un mendigo tan joven
Que sus ojos parecían dos lagos.

Me ahogué en fin, amigos;
Ahora duermo donde nunca despierto.
No saber más de mí mismo es algo triste;
Dame la guitarra para guardar las lágrimas.

Leave Me this Voice

Leave me this voice of mine,
The same one that leaves its thickets of desire
Spread out across the plain,
Its dry rivers hanging from rocks.

Let me live like a rusty sword
Without a handle, tossed up into the clouds;
I want to know nothing of the envious glory
Whose horns and tail are ashes.

I had a ring made of moonlight
Hanging in the sky at the start of autumn;
I gave it to a beggar so young
His eyes looked like two lakes.

Finally, friends, I drowned.
Now I'm sleeping where I'll never wake.
It's sad not to know myself anymore;
Give me the guitar where I can keep my tears.

PASIÓN POR PASIÓN

Pasión por pasión. Amor por amor.

Estaba en una calle de ceniza, limitada por vastos edificios de arena. Allí encontré al placer. Le miré: en sus ojos vacíos había dos relojes pequeños; uno marchaba en sentido contrario al otro. En la comisura de los labios sostenía una flor mordida. Sobre los hombros llevaba una capa en jirones.

A su paso unas estrellas se apagaban, otras se encendían. Quise detenerle; mi brazo quedó inmóvil. Lloré, lloré tanto, que hubiera podido llenar sus órbitas vacías. Entonces amaneció.

Comprendí por qué llaman prudente a un hombre sin cabeza.

Passion for Passion

Passion for passion. Love for love.

I was on a street paved with ashes, bounded by tall buildings made of sand. That's where I met pleasure. I looked into his eyes: they were empty except for two little clocks whose hands were moving in opposite directions. In his lips he was holding a bitten flower. On his shoulders he was wearing a ragged cape.

As he walked some stars went out, others came on. I tried to stop him but my arm wouldn't move. I cried, I cried so hard my tears might have filled his empty sockets. Then day broke.

I understood why they say a wise man has no head.

TU PEQUEÑA FIGURA

Tu pequeña figura, sola en algún camino,
Cae lentamente desde la luz,
Semejante a la arena desde un brazo,
Cuando la mano, poema perdido,
Abre diez estrellas sobre el otoño de rojiza resonancia.

No sabes, no sabes;
Buscas por la tierra un estremecimiento blanquecino,
Mientras los muros, con su hiedra antigua,
Crecen lentamente sobre el ocaso.

Tristeza sin guarida y sin pantano,
Sales de un frío para entrar en otro;
Abandonas la hierba tan cariñosa
Para pedir que el amor no te olvide.

Palabras de demente o palabras de muerto,
Es igual.
Escucha el agua, escucha la lluvia, escucha la tormenta;
Ésa es tu vida:
Líquido lamento fluyendo entre sombras iguales.

Your Tiny Figure

Your tiny figure, alone on some road,
Falls slowly out of the light,
Like sand from the end of an arm,
When the hand, a lost poem,
Opens ten stars over an autumn of reddish echoes.

You can't figure it out;
You search the earth for a shuddering whiteness,
While the walls, with their ancient ivy,
Grow slowly over the sunset.

Sorrow with no shelter and no marsh,
You leave one zone of cold to enter another;
You abandon the grass so tender
To ask love not to forget you.

Words of a madman or words of a dead man,
It's all the same.
Listen to the water, listen to the rain, listen to the storm;
That's your life:
A liquid lament that flows between equal shadows.

EL MIRLO, LA GAVIOTA

El mirlo, la gaviota,
El tulipán, las tuberosas,
La pampa dormida en Argentina,
El Mar Negro como después de una muerte,
Las niñitas, los tiernos niños,
Las jóvenes, el adolescente,
La mujer adulta, el hombre,
Los ancianos, las pompas fúnebres,
Van girando lentamente con el mundo;
Como si una ciruela verde,
Picoteada por el tiempo,
Fuese inconmovible en la rama.

Tiernos niñitos, yo os amo;
Os amo tanto, que vuestra madre
Creería que intentaba haceros daño.

Dame las glicinas azules sobre la tapia inocente,
Las magnolias embriagadoras sobre la falda blanca y vacía,
El libro melancólico entreabierto,
Las piernas entreabiertas,
Los bucles rubios del adolescente;
Con todo ello haré el filtro sempiterno:
Bebe unas gotas y verás la vida como a través de un vidrio
coloreado.

Déjame, ya es hora de que duerma,
De dormir este sueño inacabable.

Quiero despertar algún día,
Saber que tu pelo, niño,
Tu vientre suave y tus espaldas
No son nada, nada, nada.

Blackbird, Seagull

Blackbird, seagull,
Tulips, lilies,
The sleeping pampa in Argentina,
The Black Sea as after someone's death,
Little girls, sweet little boys,
The young, the adolescent,
The grown woman, the man,
The old, the funerals,
They go on turning slowly with the world;
As if a green plum,
Pecked by time,
Were hanging still on its branch.

Sweet little girls and boys, I love you.
I love you so much, your mother
Might think I meant you harm.

Give me cascades of blue wisteria hugging an innocent wall,
Drunkenly scented magnolias on a clean white skirt,
A melancholy book left open on a table,
Legs left open,
Blond adolescent curls—
With all these things I'll brew an eternal potion:
Sip a few drops and you'll see life through colored glass.

Now leave me alone, it's time for a nap,
Time to sleep this neverending dream.

I want to wake up someday,
Little boy, and know your hair,
Your smooth back and your belly
Are nothing, nothing at all.

Recoger conchas delicadas:
Mira qué viso violado.

Las escamas de los súbitos peces,
Los músculos dorados del marino,
Sus labios salados y frescos,
Me prenden en un mundo de espejismo.

Creo en la vida,
Creo en ti que no conozco aún,
Creo en mí mismo;
Porque algún día yo seré todas las cosas que amo:
El aire, el agua, las plantas, el adolescente.

Gather up delicate shells:
Look at their sullied gleam.

The darting fishes' scales,
The sailor's golden muscles,
His cool salty lips,
Hold me captive in a world of illusions.

I believe in life,
I believe in you though we've never met,
I believe in myself;
Because one day I'll be all the things I love:
Air, water, flower, adolescent.

COMO LEVE SONIDO

Como leve sonido:
Hoja que roza un vidrio,
Agua que pasa unas guijas,
Lluvia que besa una frente juvenil;

Como rápida caricia:
Pie desnudo sobre el camino,
Dedos que ensayan el primer amor,
Sábanas tibias sobre el cuerpo solitario;

Como fugaz deseo:
Seda brillante en la luz,
Esbelto adolescente entrevisto,
Lágrimas por ser más que un hombre;

Como esta vida que no es mía
Y sin embargo es la mía,
Como este afán sin nombre
Que no me pertenece y sin embargo soy yo;

Como todo aquello que de cerca o de lejos
Me roza, me besa, me hiere,
Tu presencia está conmigo fuera y dentro,
Es mi vida misma y no es mi vida,
Así como una hoja y otra hoja
Son la apariencia del viento que las lleva.

The Same Way a Light Sound

The same way a light sound:
A leaf grazing a window,
Water running over pebbles,
Rain kissing a young face;

The way a quick caress,
Bare feet on a path,
Fingers trying out first love,
Cool sheets against a solitary body;

The way a fleeting desire,
Flashing silk,
Glimpse of a slender youth,
Tears over being more than a man;

The way this life that isn't mine
And yet is mine,
The way this nameless yearning
That has nothing to do with me and yet is me;

The same way everything near or far
Grazes and kisses and wounds me,
Your presence is with me inside and out,
It is my very life yet not my life,
The same way a couple of leaves
Make visible the wind that sweeps them away.

TE QUIERO

Te quiero.

Te lo he dicho con el viento,
Jugueteando como animalillo en la arena
O iracundo como órgano tempestuoso;

Te lo he dicho con el sol,
Que dora desnudos cuerpos juveniles
Y sonríe en todas las cosas inocentes;

Te lo he dicho con las nubes,
Frentes melancólicas que sostienen el cielo,
Tristezas fugitivas;

Te lo he dicho con las plantas,
Leves criaturas transparentes
Que se cubren de rubor repentino;

Te lo he dicho con el agua,
Vida luminosa que vela un fondo de sombra;
Te lo he dicho con el miedo,
Te lo he dicho con la alegría,
Con el hastío, con las terribles palabras.

Pero así no me basta:
Más allá de la vida,
Quiero decírtelo con la muerte;
Más allá del amor,
Quiero decírtelo con el olvido.

I Love You

I love you.

I've told you with the wind,
Playful as a little animal in the sand
Or angry as an organ playing a storm;

I've told you with the sun,
Pouring its gold over the bodies of the young
And smiling on all innocent things;

I've told you with clouds,
Melancholy faces holding up the sky,
Fleeting sadnesses;

I've told you with plants,
Light transparent creatures
That suddenly blush;

I've told you with water,
Luminous life that veils a darker depth;
I've told you with fear,
I've told you with joy,
With disgust, with the terrible words.

But that's not enough for me:
Beyond life,
I want to tell you with death;
Beyond love,
I want to tell you with oblivion.

HABÍA EN EL FONDO DEL MAR

Había en el fondo del mar una perla y una vieja trompeta. Las sutiles capas del agua sonreían con delicadeza al pasar junto a ellas; las llamaban las dos amigas.

Había un niñito ahogado junto a un árbol de coral. Los brazos descoloridos y las ramas luminosas se enlazaban estrechamente; los llamaban los dos amantes.

Había un fragmento de rueda venida desde muy lejos y un pájaro disecado, que asombraba como elegante extranjero a los atónitos peces; les llamaban las nómadas.

Había una cola de sirena con reflejos venenosos y un muslo de adolescente, distantes la una del otro; les llamaban los enemigos.

Había una estrella, una liga de hombre, un libro deteriorado y un violín diminuto; había otras sorprendentes maravillas, y cuando el agua pasaba, rozándolas suavemente, parecía como si quisiera invitarlas a que la siguieran en cortejo centelleante.

Pero ninguna era comparable a una mano de yeso cortada. Era tan bella que decidí robarla. Desde entonces llena mis noches y mis días; me acaricia y me ama. La llamo la verdad del amor.

At the Bottom of the Ocean

At the bottom of the ocean lay a pearl and an old trumpet. Whitecaps smiled subtly as they passed over them; they called them the two friends.

There was a drowned boy next to a coral reef. His bleached arms and its luminous branches grew tightly entwined; they called them the two lovers.

There was a piece of a wheel from far away and a bird cut open, which like an elegant stranger astonished the fish; they called them the nomads.

There was a mermaid's tail with poisonous reflections and the thigh of an adolescent, far apart; they called them the enemies.

There was a star, a banded man, a battered book and a tiny violin; there were other marvelous surprises, and when the water flowed over them, softly stroking them, it seemed that it was trying to invite them to come along on its glittering current.

But none could compare to a broken plaster hand. It was so lovely I decided to steal it. And since then it fills my nights and my days; it caresses me and adores me. I call it true love.

VEÍA SENTADO

Veía sentado junto al agua
Con vago ademán de olvido,
Veía las hojas, los días, los semblantes,
El fondo siempre pálido del cielo,
Conversando indiferentes entre ellos mismos.

Veía la luz agitarse eficazmente,
Un pequeño lagarto de visita,
Las piedrecillas vanidosas
Disputando el lugar a las tristes hierbas.

Veía reinos perdidos o quizá ganados,
Veía mi juventud ni ganada ni perdida,
Veía mi cuerpo distante, tan extraño
Como yo mismo, allá en extraña hora.

Veía los canosos muros disgustados
Murmurando entre dientes sus vagas blasfemias,
Veía más allá de los muros
El mundo como can satisfecho,
Veía al inclinarme sobre la verdad
Un cuerpo que no era el cuerpo mío.

Subiendo hasta mí mismo
Aquí vive desde entonces,
Mientras aguardo que tu propia presencia
Haga inútil ese triste trabajo
De ser yo solo el amor y su imagen.

Sitting by the Water I Could See

Sitting by the water I could see,
With a vague gesture of forgetting,
I could see leaves, days, all looking alike,
Against the same pale sky,
Talking listlessly among themselves.

I could see light steadily shaking,
A little visiting lizard,
Self absorbed pebbles
Fighting over space with some sad weeds.

I could see kingdoms lost or possibly won,
I could see my youth neither won nor lost,
I could see my body a ways off, as strange
As I was myself, over there in that strange time.

I could see the disgusted walls with their gray hair
Muttering empty curses between their teeth,
I could see beyond the walls
The world like a well fed dog,
Leaning back on the truth I could see
A body that was no body of mine.

It climbed right up inside me
And lives here ever since then,
While I await your arrival
To render pointless this sorry work
Of being both love and its image.

HE VENIDO PARA VER

He venido para ver semblantes
Amables como viejas escobas,
He venido para ver las sombras
Que desde lejos me sonríen.

He venido para ver los muros
En el suelo o en pie indistintamente,
He venido para ver las cosas,
Las cosas soñolientas por aquí.

He venido para ver los mares
Dormidos en cestillo italiano,
He venido para ver las puertas,
El trabajo, los tejados, las virtudes
De color amarillo ya caduco.

He venido para ver la muerte
Y su graciosa red de cazar mariposas,
He venido para esperarte
Con los brazos un tanto en el aire,
He venido no sé por qué;
Un día abrí los ojos: he venido.

Por ello quiero saludar sin insistencia
A tantas cosas más que amables:
Los amigos de color celeste,
Los días de color variable,
La libertad del color de mis ojos;

Los niñitos de seda tan clara,
Los entierros aburridos como piedras,
La seguridad, ese insecto
Que anida en los volantes de la luz.

What I Came to See

I came to see the expressions
On faces kind as old brooms,
I came to see the distant
Shadows smiling at me.

I came to see the walls
Fallen or vaguely standing,
I came to see some things,
The dreamy things around here.

I came to see the ocean
Asleep in a little Italian basket,
I came to see doors,
Roofs, work, virtues
Of a faded yellowish color.

I came to see death
And its graceful butterfly net,
I came to wait for you
With my arms a little raised,
I don't know why I came;
One day I opened my eyes: I came.

That's why I want to offer a light salute
To so many more than likable things:
My sky blue friends,
The various colored days,
Freedom the color of my eyes;

Children of shiny silk,
Burials boring as stones,
Security, that insect
Building its nest in the wheels of light.

Adiós, dulces amantes invisibles,
Siento no haber dormido en vuestros brazos.
Vine por esos besos solamente;
Guardad los labios por si vuelvo.

Goodbye, my tender invisible lovers,
It feels like I never even slept in your arms.
I came for those kisses only;
Take care of your lips in case I come back.

from

Donde Habite el Olvido

Where Oblivion Lives

[1932–1933]

DONDE HABITE EL OLVIDO

I

Donde habite el olvido,
En los vastos jardines sin aurora;
Donde yo sólo sea
Memoria de una piedra sepultada entre ortigas
Sobre la cual el viento escapa a sus insomnios.

Donde mi nombre deje
Al cuerpo que designa en brazos de los siglos,
Donde el deseo no exista.

En esa gran región donde el amor, ángel terrible,
No esconda como acero
En mi pecho su ala,
Sonriendo lleno de gracia aérea mientras crece el tormento.

Allá donde termine este afán que exige un dueño a imagen suya,
Sometiendo a otra vida su vida,
Sin más horizonte que otros ojos frente a frente.

Donde penas y dichas no sean más que nombres,
Cielo y tierra nativos en torno de un recuerdo;
Donde al fin quede libre sin saberlo yo mismo,
Disuelto en niebla, ausencia,
Ausencia leve como carne de niño.

Allá, allá lejos;
Donde habite el olvido.

Where Oblivion Lives

I

Where oblivion lives,
In the vast gardens of darkness;
Where I will be no more
Than the memory of a stone lost in spiky weeds
Where the wind goes to escape its insomnia.

Where my name leaves
Its body destined for the arms of the centuries,
Where desire has ceased to exist.

In that great realm where love, terrible angel,
Doesn't slip its wing
Into my chest like a knifeblade,
Smiling airily as my torment grows.

Out there where this passion demands a master in its own image,
Submitting its life to another life,
With no more horizon than a face with other eyes.

Where sorrows and joys are nothing more than names,
Native land and sky around a memory;
Where at last I'll be free without even knowing it,
Mist in the fog, an absence,
A light absence like a child's flesh.

Out there, far away,
Where oblivion lives.

IV

Yo fui.

Columna ardiente, luna de primavera,
Mar dorado, ojos grandes.

Busqué lo que pensaba;
Pensé, como el amanecer en sueño lánguido,
Lo que pinta el deseo en días adolescentes.

Canté, subí,
Fui luz un día
Arrastrado en la llama.

Como un golpe de viento
Que deshace la sombra,
Caí en lo negro,
En el mundo insaciable.

He sido.

IV

I was.

Burning column, springtime moon,
Golden ocean, eyes wide open.

I searched for what I thought;
I thought, as in the dawn of a languid dream,
Of what desire paints in our adolescence.

I sang, I climbed,
I was a day of light
Dragged through the flame.

Like a gust of wind
Undone by the dark,
I fell into blackness,
Into the insatiable world.

I've been.

VI

El mar es un olvido,
Una canción, un labio;
El mar es un amante,
Fiel respuesta al deseo.

Es como un ruiseñor,
Y sus aguas son plumas,
Impulsos que levantan
A las frías estrellas.

Sus caricias son sueño,
Entreabren la muerte,
Son lunas accesibles,
Son la vida más alta.

Sobre espaldas oscuras
Las olas van gozando.

VI

The ocean is a forgetting,
A song, a pair of lips;
The ocean is a lover,
A faithful reply to desire.

It's like a nightingale,
Its waters are feathers
Tossed up into the sky
As far as the cold stars.

Its caresses are a dream,
An opening door into death,
They're moons that you can touch,
They're life in its highest form.

On human backs in darkness
Waves are taking their pleasure.

VII

Adolescente fui en días idénticos a nubes,
Cosa grácil, visible por penumbra y reflejo,
Y extraño es, si ese recuerdo busco,
Que tanto, tanto duela sobre el cuerpo de hoy.

Perder placer es triste
Como la dulce lámpara sobre el lento nocturno;
Aquél fui, aquél fui, aquél he sido;
Era la ignorancia mi sombra.

Ni gozo ni pena; fui niño
Prisionero entre muros cambiantes;
Historias como cuerpos, cristales como cielos,
Sueño luego, un sueño más alto que la vida.

Cuando la muerte quiera
Una verdad quitar de entre mis manos,
Las hallará vacías, como en la adolescencia
Ardientes de deseo, tendidas hacia el aire.

VII

I was an adolescent in days like clouds,
Graceful, visible in different lights,
And it's strange when I try to remember
How much this hurts my body here and now.

Pleasure lost is sad
Like a sweet lamp at nightfall;
That's who I was, that's who I was, I was;
Ignorance was my shadow.

No pleasure, no pain; I was a boy
Imprisoned between shifting walls;
Stories like bodies, windows like skies,
Then sleep, a sleep higher than life itself.

When death tries
To take a truth out of my hands,
It will find them empty, as in adolescence
Ardent with desire, held in the air.

IX

Era un sueño, aire
Tranquilo en la nada;
Al abrir los ojos
Las ramas perdían.

Exhalaba el tiempo
Luces vegetales,
Amores caídos,
Tristeza sin donde.

Volvía la sombra;
Agua eran sus labios.
Cristal, soledades,
La frente, la lámpara.

Pasión sin figura,
Pena sin historia;
Como herida al pecho,
Un beso, el deseo.

No sabes, no sabes.

IX

It was a dream, just air
Calm in its nothingness,
Your eyes opening
Lost their limbs.

Time breathed out
A plantlike light,
Fallen loves,
Sorrow from who knows where.

Then darkness returned;
Its mouth was water,
Crystal, solitudes,
A face, a lamp.

Passion without a form,
Grief without a story;
Like a wounded heart,
A kiss, a desire.

You'll never understand.

XI

No quiero, triste espíritu, volver
Por los lugares que cruzó mi llanto,
Latir secreto entre los cuerpos vivos
Como yo también fui.

No quiero recordar
Un instante feliz entre tormentos;
Goce o pena, es igual,
Todo es triste al volver.

Aún va conmigo como una luz lejana
Aquel destino niño,
Aquellos dulces ojos juveniles,
Aquella antigua herida.

No, no quisiera volver,
Sino morir aún más,
Arrancar una sombra,
Olvidar un olvido.

XI

No, sad spirit, don't take me back
Through all those places my crying crossed,
To throb secretly between bodies alive
As I myself once was.

I don't want to remember
One happy moment among the sufferings;
Pain or pleasure, it's all the same,
Everything's sad when you go back.

But like a distant light that child's fate
Comes with me still,
Those tender youthful eyes,
That ancient wound.

No, I don't want to go back,
But to die even deeper,
To tear out the roots of a shadow,
To forget what's forgotten.

XII

No es el amor quien muere,
Somos nosotros mismos.

Inocencia primera
Abolida en deseo,
Olvido de sí mismo en otro olvido,
Ramas entrelazadas,
¿Por qué vivir si desaparecéis un día?

Sólo vive quien mira
Siempre ante sí los ojos de su aurora,
Sólo vive quien besa
Aquel cuerpo de ángel que el amor levantara.

Fantasmas en la pena,
A lo lejos, los otros,
Los que ese amor perdieron,
Como un recuerdo en sueños,
Recorriendo las tumbas
Otro vacío estrechan.

Por allá van y gimen,
Muertos en pie, vidas tras de la piedra,
Golpeando impotencia,
Arañando la sombra
Con inútil ternura.

No, no es el amor quien muere.

XII

It isn't love that dies,
It is we ourselves.

Original innocence
Abolished by desire,
Forgetting yourself in another forgetting,
Intertwined limbs,
Why live if you're doomed to disappear?

He alone is alive who sees
Always before him the eyes of his sunrise,
He alone is alive who kisses
That angelic body love has erected.

Phantoms of grief,
Far off, the others,
The ones who lost that love,
Like memory in dreams,
Grazing the graves
Embrace another void.

Out there they go on moaning,
The walking dead, lives locked in stone,
Pounding at impotence,
Scratching at darkness
With useless tenderness.

No, it isn't love that dies.

XIV

A Concha Méndez
y Manuel Altolaguirre

Eras tierno deseo, nube insinuante,
Vivías con el aire entre cuerpos amigos,
Alentabas sin forma, sonreías sin voz,
Dejo inspirado de invisible espíritu.

Nuestra impotencia, lenta espina,
Quizá en ti hubiera sido fuerza adolescente;
No dolor irrisorio ni placer egoísta,
No sueño de una vida ni maldad triunfante.

Como nube feliz que pasa sin la lluvia,
Como un ave olvidada de la rama nativa,
A un tiempo poseíste muerte y vida,
Sin haber muerto, sin haber vivido.

Entre el humo tan triste, entre las flacas calles
De una tierra medida por los odios antiguos,
No has descubierto así, vueltos contra tu dicha,
El poder con sus manos de fango,
Un dios abyecto disponiendo destinos,
La mentira y su cola redonda erguida sobre el mundo,
El inerme amor llorando entre las tumbas.

Tu leve ausencia, eco sin nota, tiempo sin historia,
Pasando igual que un ala,
Deja una verdad transparente;
Verdad que supo y no sintió,
Verdad que vio y no quiso.

XIV

for Concha Méndez
and Manuel Altolaguirre

You were tender desire, clever cloud,
You lived in the air between friendly bodies,
You breathed without form, you smiled without speech,
Inspired trace of invisible spirit.

Our helplessness, long thorn,
Perhaps in you it might have been the strength of adolescence;
Neither a painful joke nor selfish pleasure,
Neither a dream of life nor evil triumphant.

Like a happy cloud floating by without rain,
Like a bird that's forgotten the branch where it was born,
At one time you possessed both death and life,
Never having died nor having lived.

In the sad smoke, in the narrow streets
Of a land measured by its ancient hatreds,
You've never discovered, turned against your luck,
Power with its filthy hands,
A pitiful god dealing out destinies,
The great lie with its long tail wrapped around the world,
Defenseless love weeping over the graves.

Your light absence, echo of no note, time without a story,
Passing like a wing,
Leaves one transparent truth;
A truth it knew and never felt,
A truth it saw and didn't want.

XV

El invisible muro
Entre los brazos todos,
Entre los cuerpos todos,
Islas de maldad irrisoria.

No hay besos, sino losas;
No hay amor, sino losas
Tantas veces medidas por el paso
Febril del prisionero.

Quizá el aire afuera
Suene cantando al mundo
El himno de la fiel alegría;
Quizá, glorias enajenadas,
Alas radiantes pasan.

Un deseo inmenso,
Afán de una verdad,
Bate contra los muros,
Bate contra la carne
Como un mar entre hierros.

Ávidos un momento
Unos ojos se alzan
Hacia el rayo del día,
Relámpago cobrizo victorioso
Con su espada tan alta.

Entre piedras de sombra,
De ira, llanto, olvido,
Alienta la verdad.

La prisión,
La prisión viva.

XV

The invisible wall
Between all arms,
Between all bodies,
Islands of laughable evil.

No kisses, just stone slabs;
No love, just slabs
Measured so many times
By the prisoner's feverish steps.

Perhaps the air outside
Sounds like the world singing
Its hymn of faithful joy;
Maybe long gone glories
And radiant wings go by.

Some immense desire,
Passion for some truth,
Pounds the walls,
Pounds the flesh
Like an ocean against its bars.

Eager for a moment,
Some eyes look up
Toward the first light of day,
Triumphant coppery lightning
With its sword raised high.

Amid stones of darkness,
Of rage, crying, forgetting,
The truth breathes.

The prison,
The prison of living.

LOS FANTASMAS DEL DESEO

A Bernabé Fernández-Canivell

Yo no te conocía, tierra;
Con los ojos inertes, la mano aleteante,
Lloré todo ciego bajo tu verde sonrisa,
Aunque, alentar juvenil, sintiera a veces
Un tumulto sediento de postrarse,
Como huracán henchido aquí en el pecho;
Ignorándote, tierra mía,
Ignorando tu alentar, huracán o tumulto,
Idénticos en esta melancólica burbuja que yo soy
A quien tu voz de acero inspirara un menudo vivir.

Bien sé ahora que tú eres
Quien me dicta esta forma y este ansia;
Sé al fin que el mar esbelto,
La enamorada luz, los niños sonrientes,
No son sino tú misma;
Que los vivos, los muertos,
El placer y la pena,
La soledad, la amistad,
La miseria, el poderoso estúpido,
El hombre enamorado, el canalla,
Son tan dignos de mí como de ellos yo lo soy;
Mis brazos, tierra, son ya más anchos, ágiles,
Para llevar tu afán que nada satisface.

El amor no tiene esta o aquella forma,
No puede detenerse en criatura alguna;
Todas son por igual viles y soñadoras.
Placer que nunca muere,
Beso que nunca muere,
Sólo en ti misma encuentro, tierra mía.

Phantoms of Desire

for Bernabé Fernández-Canivell

I never knew you, earth;
With my useless eyes, my fluttering hands,
I cried in my blindness under your green smile,
Even though, in my childish breathing, I could feel at times
A turbulence thirsting to be humbled,
Like a hurricane churning in my chest;
Not knowing you, my earth,
Not knowing your breathing hurricane turbulence,
Just like this melancholy bubble I've become
That your steel voice might have inspired to live a little.

Now I know that you're the one
Who gave me this form, this longing;
Finally I know the slender ocean,
The enamored light, the smiling boys,
Are nothing more than yourself;
That the living, the dead,
Pleasure and grief,
Friendship, solitude,
Misery, the stupid boss,
The man in love, the lowlife,
Are as worthy of me as I of them:
My arms, earth, are spread still wider, stronger,
The better to hold your insatiable hunger.

Love doesn't take just this or that form,
It never really stays in any being;
We are all equally vile and dreamy.
Pleasure that never dies,
Kisses that never die,
I find them in no one but you, my earth.

Nimbos de juventud, cabellos rubios o sombríos,
Rizosos o lánguidos como una primavera,
Sobre cuerpos cobrizos, sobre radiantes cuerpos
Que tanto he amado inútilmente,
No es en vosotros donde la vida está, sino en la tierra,
En la tierra que aguarda, aguarda siempre
Con sus labios tendidos, con sus brazos abiertos.

Dejadme, dejadme abarcar, ver unos instantes
Este mundo divino que ahora es mío,
Mío como lo soy yo mismo,
Como lo fueron otros cuerpos que estrecharon mis brazos,
Como la arena, que al besarla los labios
Finge otros labios, dúctiles al deseo,
Hasta que el viento lleva sus mentirosos átomos.

Como la arena, tierra,
Como la arena misma,
La caricia es mentira, el amor es mentira, la amistad es mentira.
Tú sola quedas con el deseo,
Con este deseo que aparenta ser mío y ni siquiera es mío,
Sino el deseo de todos,
Malvados, inocentes,
Enamorados o canallas.

Tierra, tierra y deseo.
Una forma perdida.

Auras of youth, dark or blond hair,
Curly or straight like springtime
On coppery bodies, on radiant bodies
I've loved so much so uselessly,
Life is not in you but in the earth,
In the faithful earth that waits forever
With its parted lips, with its open arms.

Just let me hold them and know for a few moments
This divine world that is mine for now,
Mine as I myself am,
As were other bodies that my arms once held,
Like sand kissed by my lips
That pretends to be other lips yielding to desire
Until the wind blows away all its lying grains.

Like sand, earth,
Like sand itself,
Caresses are a lie, love is a lie, friendship a lie.
You alone stay true to desire,
This desire that feels like mine and isn't mine,
But everyone's desire,
The wicked, the innocent,
Lovers, lowlifes.

Earth, earth and desire.
A lost embodiment.

from

Invocaciones
Invocations
[1934–1935]

A UN MUCHACHO ANDALUZ

Te hubiera dado el mundo,
Muchacho que surgiste
Al caer de la luz por tu Conquero,
Tras la colina ocre,
Entre pinos antiguos de perenne alegría.

¿Eras emanación del mar cercano?
Eras el mar aún más
Que las aguas henchidas con su aliento,
Encauzadas en río sobre tu tierra abierta,
Bajo el inmenso cielo con nubes que se orlaban de rotos
resplandores.

Eras el mar aún más
Tras de las pobres telas que ocultaban tu cuerpo;
Eras forma primera,
Eras fuerza inconsciente de su propia hermosura.

Y tus labios, de bisel tan terso,
Eran la vida misma,
Como una ardiente flor
Nutrida con la savia
De aquella piel oscura
Que infiltraba nocturno escalofrío.

Si el amor fuera un ala.

La incierta hora con nubes desgarradas,
El río oscuro y ciego bajo la extraña brisa,
La rojiza colina con sus pinos cargados de secretos,
Te enviaban a mí, a mi afán ya caído,
Como verdad tangible.

To an Andalusian Boy

I would have given you everything,
Boy who appeared
When light fell on your landscape
Behind the ochre hill
Down through the old and always happy pines.

Were you an emanation of the ocean?
You were even more ocean
Than the deep breathing waters
Flowing downriver over your open land
Under a huge sky whose clouds are bordered by a broken
    radiance.

Your were even more ocean
Under the poor clothes covering your body;
You were a primal form,
You were a force unconscious of your own beauty.

And your lips, so smoothly beveled,
Were life itself,
Like a burning blossom
Nourished with the sap
Of that dark skin
Filled with the chill of night.

If only love were a wing.

The uncertain hour with its ragged clouds,
The blind, dark river under its strange breeze,
The pink hillside with its pines full of secrets,
Sent you to me, to my fallen passion,
Like a tangible truth.

Expresión armoniosa de aquel mismo paraje,
Entre los ateridos fantasmas que habitan nuestro mundo,
Eras tú una verdad,
Sola verdad que busco,
Más que verdad de amor, verdad de vida;
Y olvidando que sombra y pena acechan de continuo
Esa cúspide virgen de la luz y la dicha,
Quise por un momento fijar tu curso ineluctable.

Creí en ti, muchachillo.

Cuando el mar evidente,
Con el irrefutable sol de mediodía,
Suspendía mi cuerpo
En esa abdicación del hombre ante su dios,
Un resto de memoria
Levantaba tu imagen como recuerdo único.

Y entonces,
Con sus luces el violento Atlántico,
Tantas dunas profusas, tu Conquero nativo,
Estaban en mí mismo dichos en tu figura,
Divina ya para mi afán con ellos,
Porque nunca he querido dioses crucificados,
Tristes dioses que insultan
Esa tierra ardorosa que te hizo y deshace.

Harmonious expression of that very place,
Among the shivering phantoms who fill our world
You were a truth,
The only truth I want,
More than the truth of love, the truth of life;
And forgetting darkness and grief perpetually threaten
That virgin crest of life and happiness,
I tried to hold your ceaseless flow for a moment.

I believed in you, kid.

When the obvious ocean
Under the irrefutable sun of noon
Held my body
In that surrender of a man to his god,
A trace of memory
Raised up your image like the only evidence.

And then
The violent Atlantic with its lights,
So many rolling dunes, your native terrain,
Were spoken through your figure into me,
Now godlike in my passion for them,
Because crucified gods were never what I wanted,
Sad gods who abuse
That ardent land, which made you and breaks you down.

SOLILOQUIO DEL FARERO

Cómo llenarte, soledad,
Sino contigo misma.

De niño, entre las pobres guaridas de la tierra,
Quieto en ángulo oscuro,
Buscaba en ti, encendida guirnalda,
Mis auroras futuras y furtivos nocturnos,
Y en ti los vislumbraba,
Naturales y exactos, también libres y fieles,
A semejanza mía,
A semejanza tuya, eterna soledad.

Me perdí luego por la tierra injusta
Como quien busca amigos o ignorados amantes;
Diverso con el mundo,
Fui luz serena y anhelo desbocado,
Y en la lluvia sombría o en el sol evidente
Quería una verdad que a ti te traicionase,
Olvidando en mi afán
Cómo las alas fugitivas su propia nube crean.

Y al velarse a mis ojos
Con nubes sobre nubes de otoño desbordado
La luz de aquellos días en ti misma entrevistos,
Te negué por bien poco;
Por menudos amores ni ciertos ni fingidos,
Por quietas amistades de sillón y de gesto,
Por un nombre de reducida cola en un mundo fantasma,
Por los viejos placeres prohibidos,
Como los permitidos nauseabundos,
Útiles solamente para el elegante salón susurrado,
En bocas de mentira y palabras de hielo.

The Lighthouse Keeper's Soliloquy

How else to fill you, solitude,
Except with yourself.

As a boy, in little shelters in the ground,
Quietly crouching in the dark,
I sought in you, burning garland,
My future dawns and furtive nights,
And in you I could make them out,
Life size and precise, and freely faithful,
In my own image,
In your image, eternal solitude.

Later I was lost over the unjust earth
Like someone in search of friends or unknown lovers;
Scattered about the world
I was pure light and unleashed desire,
And under dark rain or in full sun
I wanted a truth that would betray you,
Forgetting in my zeal
How wings in flight create their own clouds.

And my sight obscured
By layers of those overflowing autumn clouds
From the light of those days where I glimpsed you truly,
I renounced you for a while;
In little affairs neither true nor false,
In casual drawing room friendships,
In the streak of a name across a phantom world,
In the old forbidden pleasures,
Like the sickening permitted ones
Acceptable in elegantly murmuring salons
Where lying mouths whisper frigid words.

Por ti me encuentro ahora el eco de la antigua persona
Que yo fui,
Que yo mismo manché con aquellas juveniles traiciones;
Por ti me encuentro ahora, constelados hallazgos,
Limpios de otro deseo,
El sol, mi dios, la noche rumorosa,
La lluvia, intimidad de siempre,
El bosque y su alentar pagano,
El mar, el mar como su nombre hermoso;
Y sobre todos ellos,
Cuerpo oscuro y esbelto,
Te encuentro a ti, tú, soledad tan mía,
Y tú me das fuerza y debilidad
Como al ave cansada los brazos de la piedra.

Acodado al balcón miro insaciable el oleaje,
Oigo sus oscuras imprecaciones,
Contemplo sus blancas caricias;
Y erguido desde cuna vigilante
Soy en la noche un diamante que gira advirtiendo a los hombres,
Por quienes vivo, aun cuando no los vea;
Y así, lejos de ellos,
Ya olvidados sus nombres, los amo en muchedumbres,
Roncas y violentas como el mar, mi morada,
Puras ante la espera de una revolución ardiente
O rendidas y dóciles, como el mar sabe serlo
Cuando toca la hora de reposo que su fuerza conquista.

Tú, verdad solitaria,
Transparente pasión, mi soledad de siempre,
Eres inmenso abrazo;
El sol, el mar,
La oscuridad, la estepa,

In you I now find the echo of that old person
I was,
The one I stained with those youthful betrayals;
Through you I now meet myself clean of any other desire,
Gathered by chance with
My god the sun, rustling night,
Rain, my faithful intimate,
The woods in their pagan breathing,
The ocean, the ocean like its gorgeous name;
And above all of them,
Dark slender body,
I find you, my selfsame solitude,
And you give me strength and weakness,
Like the rock's open arms to the tired bird.

Leaning on the balcony I watch the insatiable waves,
I hear their dark curses,
I see their white caresses,
And erect, awake in my cradle,
I am a burning diamond turning its warning for the men
I live for, though I can't see them;
And so, far from them,
Their names forgotten, I love them in crowds,
Rough and violent as the ocean, my home,
Pure before the hope of a burning revolution
Or peacefully surrendered, as the sea can be
In the calm that follows a conquest.

You, solitary truth,
Bright passion, my faithful solitude,
Are a vast embrace;
Sun, ocean,
Darkness, plain,

El hombre y su deseo,
La airada muchedumbre,
¿Qué son sino tú misma?

Por ti, mi soledad, los busqué un día;
En ti, mi soledad, los amo ahora.

Man and his desire,
Angry mob,
What are they if not you?

Because of you, my solitude, I sought them once;
In you, my solitude, I love them now.

EL VIENTO DE SEPTIEMBRE ENTRE LOS CHOPOS

Por este clima lúcido,
Furor estival muerto,
Mi vano afán persigue
Un algo entre los bosques.

Un no sé qué, una sombra,
Cuerpo de mi deseo,
Arbórea dicha acaso
Junto a un río tranquilo.

Pero escucho; resuena
Por el aire delgado,
Estelar melodía,
Un eco entre los chopos.

Oigo caricias leves,
Oigo besos más leves;
Por allá baten alas,
Por allá van secretos.

No, vosotros no sois,
Arroyos taciturnos,
Frágiles amoríos
Como de sombra humana.

No, clara juventud,
No juguéis mi destino;
No busco vuestra gracia
Ni esa breve sonrisa.

Corre allí, entre las cañas,
Susurrante armonía;

September Wind in the Poplars

In this clear weather,
Summer's excitement over,
My vain desire's still chasing
Something through the woods.

A who knows what, a shadow,
Body of my desire,
A leafy joy somehow
Near a serene river.

But listen; an echo,
A starlike melody
In slender air
Sounds among the poplars.

I can hear soft caresses,
I can hear softer kisses;
Wings beating over there,
Secrets moving here.

No, you don't even exist,
Quiet streams and hollows,
Fragile fallings in love
As if with human shadows.

No, luminous youth,
You don't play with my fate;
I'm not in search of that grace
Nor that brief smile's mouth.

Run down there, in the reeds,
Whispering harmony;

Canta una voz, cantando
Como yo mismo, lejos.

Hundo mi cabellera,
Busco labios, miradas,
Tras las inquietas hojas
De estos cuerpos esbeltos.

Ávido aspiro sombra;
Oigo un afán tan mío.
Canta, deseo, canta
La canción de mi dicha.

Altas sombras mortales:
Vida, afán, canto, os dejo.
Quiero anegar mi espíritu
Hecho gloria amarilla.

A voice is singing, singing
Like mine, a little ways off.

I'm letting down my hair,
I'm looking for lips, glances,
Behind the restless leaves
Of these slender bodies.

I take deep breaths of darkness;
I hear my own desire.
Sing, my longing, sing
The song of my happiness.

You tall mortal shadows:
I leave you life, desire, song.
I want my spirit submerged
And turned to yellow glory.

NO ES NADA, ES UN SUSPIRO

No es nada, es un suspiro,
Pero nunca sació nadie esa nada
Ni nadie supo nunca de qué alta roca nace.

Ni puedes tú saberlo, tú que eres
Nuestro afán, nuestro amor,
Nuestra angustia de hombres;
Palabra que creamos
En horas de dolor solitario.

Un suspiro no es nada,
Como tampoco es nada
El viento entre los chopos,
La bruma sobre el mar
O ese impulso que guía
Un cuerpo hacia otro cuerpo.

Nada mi fe, mi llama,
Ni este vivir oscuro que la lleva;
Su latido o su ardor
No son sino un suspiro,
Aire triste o risueño
Con el viento que escapa.

Sombra, si tú lo sabes, dime;
Deja el hondo fluir
Libre sobre su margen invisible,
Acuérdate del hombre que suspira
Antes de que la luz vele su muerte,
Vuelto él también latir de aire,
Suspiro entre tus manos poderosas.

It's Nothing, Just a Sigh

It's nothing, just a sigh,
But no one was ever satisfied with this nothing
And no one ever knew what cliff it fell from.

Nor can you understand it, you
Our desire, our love,
Our anguish over men;
Words that we set down
In hours of lonely pain.

A sigh is nothing at all,
The same way wind
In poplars is nothing at all,
Or mist on the ocean
Or that impulse that draws
Two bodies together.

My faith, my flame are nothing,
Nor this dark life that bears them;
Its heartbeat or its passion
Are no more than a sigh,
A happy or sad tune
Floating away on the wind.

Darkness, if you know, tell me;
Set free the deeper stream
Across your invisible boundary,
Attune yourself with the sighing
Man who is not yet dead,
He too just a breath of air,
A sigh in your powerful hands.

POR UNOS TULIPANES AMARILLOS

Tragando sueño tras un vidrio impalpable,
Entre las dobles fauces,
Tuyas, pereza, de ti también, costumbre,
Vivía en un país del claro sur
Cuando a mí vino, alegre mensaje de algún dios,
No sé qué aroma joven,
Hálito henchido de tibieza prematura.

No se advertía el eco de un remoto clima celeste
En la figura del etéreo visitante,
Veíamos tan sólo
Una luz virgen, pétalo voluptuoso toda ella,
Que ondulaba en sus manos bajo la sonrisa insegura,
Como si temiera a la tierra.

Con gesto enamorado
Me adelantó los tiernos fulgores vegetales,
Sosteniendo su goteante claridad,
Forma llena de seducción terrestre,
En unos densos tulipanes amarillos
Erguidos como dichas entre verdes espadas.

Por un aletear de labio a labio
Sellé el pacto, unidos el cielo con la tierra,
Y entonces la vida abrió los ojos sin malicia,
Con absorta delicadeza, como niño reciente.

Tendido en la yacija del mortal más sombrío
Tuve tus alas, rubio mensajero,
En transporte de ternura y rencor entremezclado;
Y mordí duramente la verdad del amor, para que no pasara
Y palpitara fija

All for Some Yellow Tulips

Swallowing sleep behind a pane of impalpable glass,
Between the twin throats
Of laziness and custom,
I was living in a country in the bright south
When some god's happy message struck me,
Some young scent,
A brimming breath of unexpected warmth.

It wasn't the trace of some faraway heavenly climate announcing
  itself
In the form of an ethereal visitor,
All we saw
Was a virgin light, a vast voluptuous petal
Vibrating in its hands under a shy smile,
As if it were afraid of the earth.

With a loving gesture
It held out toward me tender flares of vegetation,
Lifting their dripping brightness
In a form full of earthy seduction,
A dense patch of yellow tulips
Erect like luck amid blades of green.

My lips brushed theirs
Sealing our pact, the sky and earth made one,
And then life's eyes could open without malice,
Gently entranced like a young child.

Lying on a bed of mortal darkness
I took your wings, blond messenger,
In a transport of tenderness mixed with anger;
And I bit hard into the truth of love, so it wouldn't pass
And would throb forever

En la memoria de alguien,
Amante, dios o la muerte en su día.

Arrastrado en la ráfaga,
Al cobrar pie entre los mirtos misteriosos
Que sustentan la tierra con su terco alimento de sombras,
El claro visitante ya no estaba,
Sólo una ligera embriaguez por la casa vacía.

Mas todavía, sobre el cristal acuoso,
Con esos bajos rayos que vierte un sol aterido,
Los tulipanes de bordes requemados
Dejaban escapar el terso espíritu.

Dura melancolía,
No en vano nos has criado con venenosa leche,
Siempre tu núcleo seco
Tropiezan nuestros dientes en la elástica carne de la dicha,
Como semilla en la pulpa coloreada de algún fruto.
¿Dónde ocultar mi vida como un remordimiento?

Tú, lluvia que entierras este día primero de la ausencia,
Como si nada ni nadie hubiera de amar más,
Dame tierra, una llama, que traguen puramente
Esas flores borrosas,
Y con ellas
El peso de una dicha hurtada al rígido destino.

In someone's memory,
Lover, god, or death in its day.

Knocked down by lightning,
When I stood up again in the mysterious myrtle
Nourishing the land with its tough diet of darkness,
The bright visitor was gone,
Leaving a light dizziness adrift in the empty house.

Yet still, on the wet window,
In those slanted rays the sun spills going down,
The tulips with their singed edges
Let their fluid spirit escape.

Hard melancholy,
You haven't nursed us on your venomous milk in vain,
Our teeth biting into the flesh of happiness
Always met your dry pit
Like a stone in the pink pulp of some fruit.
Where can I hide this lifelong regret?

You, rain that buries the first day of his absence
As if nothing and no one could ever love again,
Give me land and a flame to swallow whole
Those blurry flowers
And with them
The weight of a happiness swept away by fate.

LA GLORIA DEL POETA

Demonio hermano mío, mi semejante,
Te vi palidecer, colgado como la luna matinal,
Oculto en una nube por el cielo,
Entre las horribles montañas,
Una llama a guisa de flor tras la menuda oreja tentadora,
Blasfemando lleno de dicha ignorante,
Igual que un niño cuando entona su plegaria,
Y burlándote cruelmente al contemplar mi cansancio de
la tierra.

Mas no eres tú,
Amor mío hecho eternidad,
Quien deba reír de este sueño, de esta impotencia, de esta caída,
Porque somos chispas de un mismo fuego
Y un mismo soplo nos lanzó sobre las ondas tenebrosas
De una extraña creación, donde los hombres
Se acaban como un fósforo al trepar los fatigosos años de
sus vidas.

Tu carne como la mía
Desea tras el agua y el sol el roce de la sombra;
Nuestra palabra anhela
El muchacho semejante a una rama florida
Que pliega la gracia de su aroma y color en el aire cálido
de mayo;
Nuestros ojos el mar monótono y diverso,
Poblado por el grito de las aves grises en la tormenta,
Nuestra mano hermosos versos que arrojar al desdén de
los hombres.

Los hombres tú los conoces, hermano mío;
Míralos cómo enderezan su invisible corona
Mientras se borran en la sombra con sus mujeres al brazo,

The Poet's Glory

My demon brother, my spitting image,
I saw you faded, hanging in the sky like a moon at dawn
Hidden in a cloud
Between horrible mountains,
A flowerlike flame, your tongue at my ear,
Whispering curses full of ignorant happiness,
Just like a little boy saying his prayers,
And laughing at how sick I am of this earth.

But it's not you,
My love turned eternal,
Who should be laughing at this dream, this impotence, this
  expulsion,
Because you and I are sparks of the same fire
And a selfsame breath launched us onto the dark waves
Of a strange creation, where men
Burn out like matches mounting the exhausting years of their
  lives.

Your flesh like mine
After sun and water craves the caress of shade;
What arouses our words
Is the boy who resembles a flowering branch
Gracefully unfolding its blossoms and scent in the warm May air;
The constantly changing ocean full of the cries of gray gulls in a
  storm
Is what moves our eyes,
And our hands are moved to write beautiful poems we publish
  for men's contempt.

You know men, my dear brother;
See how they straighten their invisible crown,
Erased as they are in their women's shadow,

Carga de suficiencia inconsciente,
Llevando a comedida distancia del pecho,
Como sacerdotes católicos la forma de su triste dios,
Los hijos conseguidos a unos minutos que se hurtaron al sueño
Para dedicarlos a la cohabitación, en la densa tiniebla conyugal
De sus cubiles, escalonados los unos sobre los otros.

Mírales perdidos en la naturaleza,
Cómo enferman entre los graciosos castaños o los taciturnos
plátanos.
Cómo levantan con avaricia el mentón,
Sintiendo un miedo oscuro morderles los talones;
Mira cómo desertan de su trabajo el séptimo día autorizado,
Mientras la caja, el mostrador, la clínica, el bufete, el despacho
oficial
Dejan pasar el aire con callado rumor por su ámbito solitario.

Escúchales brotar interminables palabras
Aromatizadas de facilidad violenta,
Reclamando un abrigo para el niñito encadenado bajo el
sol divino
O una bebida tibia, que resguarde aterciopeladamente
El clima de sus fauces,
A quienes dañaría la excesiva frialdad del agua natural.

Oye sus marmóreos preceptos
Sobre lo útil, lo normal y lo hermoso;
Óyeles dictar la ley al mundo, acotar el amor, dar canon a la
belleza inexpresable,
Mientras deleitan sus sentidos con altavoces delirantes;
Contempla sus extraños cerebros
Intentando levantar, hijo a hijo, un complicado edificio
de arena
Que negase con torva frente lívida la refulgente paz de
las estrellas.

Weighed down with oblivious self-satisfaction
Worn a comfortable distance from the heart
As Catholic priests wear the sad little form of their god,
Conceiving children in a few moments stolen from sleep
So they can devote themselves to living together in the conjugal
darkness
Of their cages stacked one atop the other.

Look at them getting lost out in the country,
Feeling ill at ease amid the elegant chestnuts or taciturn
plane trees.
How they keep their chin up with such ambition,
Feeling a dark fear snapping at their heels;
See how they take the seventh day off as permitted,
While the counter, the cash register, the clinic, the desk,
the office
Can feel the fresh air rustling through their desolate spaces.

Listen to them spouting their interminable words
Perfumed with a violent self-assurance,
Forcing an overcoat on the little boy in chains under the
divine sun,
Or a warm drink, gentle on the throat
Going down,
For those who can't take water's natural chill.

Hear their commandments carved in marble
On what they call useful, normal, beautiful;
Hear how they dictate laws to the world, try to limit love, define
inexpressible beauty,
While their senses revel in the sound of delirious loudspeakers;
Consider their strange minds
Attempting to build, child by child, a complex sandcastle
That might deny with its frightful façade the shining peace of
the stars.

Ésos son, hermano mío,
Los seres con quienes muero a solas,
Fantasmas que harían brotar un día
El solemne erudito, oráculo de estas palabras mías ante
  alumnos extraños,
Obteniendo por ello renombre,
Más una pequeña casa de campo en la angustiosa sierra
  inmediata a la capital;
En tanto tú, tras irisada niebla,
Acaricias los rizos de tu cabellera
Y contemplas con gesto distraído desde la altura
Esta sucia tierra donde el poeta se ahoga.

Sabes sin embargo que mi voz es la tuya,
Que mi amor es el tuyo;
Deja, oh, deja por una larga noche
Resbalar tu cálido cuerpo oscuro,
Ligero como un látigo,
Bajo el mío, momia de hastío sepulta en anónima yacija,
Y que tus besos, ese venero inagotable,
Viertan en mí la fiebre de una pasión a muerte entre los dos;
Porque me cansa la vana tarea de las palabras,
Como al niño las dulces piedrecillas
Que arroja a un lago, para ver estremecerse su calma
Con el reflejo de una gran ala misteriosa.

Es hora ya, es más que tiempo
De que tus manos cedan a mi vida
El amargo puñal codiciado del poeta;
De que lo hundas, con sólo un golpe limpio,
En este pecho sonoro y vibrante, idéntico a un laúd,
Donde la muerte únicamente,
La muerte únicamente,
Puede hacer resonar la melodía prometida.

Those are the very ones, my brother,
The people with whom I'm dying all alone,
Phantoms that will give rise one day
To the solemn pedant trained to explain my words to his
   bored students,
And getting a little famous,
With a house in the capital's anxious foothills;
Just as you, behind your hazy rainbow,
Run your fingers through your long curls
And look down with a distracted expression
On this filthy earth where a poet is going under.

And yet you also know my voice is yours,
My love is yours;
Ah for just one long night
Let your warm dark body slip
Light as a whip
Underneath mine, a rotting mummy buried in some
   unmarked grave,
And let the bottomless spring of your kisses
Pour into me the fever of a passion gone dead between us;
Because I'm sick of the vain labor of words,
Like a boy skipping his sweet little stones over a lake
Merely to send a ripple through its stillness
Like the shadow of some great mysterious wing.

Now is the time, it's long past time
For your hands to plunge into my life
The poet's coveted and bitter knife—
One clean stroke through the heart,
Resonant and trembling like a lute
Where only death
And death alone
Can make the promised melody resound.

EL JOVEN MARINO

El mar, y nada más.

Insaciable, insaciable.
Con pie desnudo ibas sobre la olvidadiza arena,
Dulcemente trastornado, como el hombre cuando un
placer espera,
Tu cabello seguía la invocación frenética del viento;
Todo tú vuelto apasionado albatros,
A quien su trágico desear brotaba en alas,
Al único maestro respondías:
El mar, única criatura
Que pudiera asumir tu vida poseyéndote.

Tuyo sólo en los ojos no te bastaba,
Ni en el ligero abrazo del nadador indiferente;
Lo querías aún más:
Sus infalibles labios transparentes contra los tuyos ávidos,
Tu quebrada cintura contra el argénteo escudo de su vientre,
Y la vida escapando,
Como sangre sin cárcel,
Desde el fatal olvido en que caías.

Ahí estás ya.
No puedes recordar,
Porque ahora tú mismo eres quieto recuerdo;
Y aquella remota belleza,
En tu cuerpo cifrada como feliz columna,
Hoy sólo alienta en mí,
En mí que la revivo bajo esta oscura forma,
Que cuando tú vivías
Sobre un ara invisible te adivinaba erguido.

Young Man of the Sea

The ocean, nothing else.

Insatiable, insatiable.
You walked barefoot over the oblivious sand,
Your hair gently writhing under the wind's rough influence
Like someone anticipating pleasure;
Turned into an albatross of passion,
Its tragic longing breaking out in wings,
You answered your only master:
The ocean, the only creation
That could ever possess your life.

To have it in sight was not enough for you,
Nor in the light embrace of the casual swimmer;
You wanted more:
Its perfect lucid lips thirstily pressed to yours,
Your broken waist against the silvery shield of its belly,
Your life escaping
Like blood set free
From the deadly forgetting where you fell.

There you are still.
You don't remember,
Because now you are nothing but a mute memory;
And that remote beauty,
Encoded in your body as in a pillar,
Now breathes only in me,
In me who resurrects it in this obscure form,
Who when you lived
Imagined you on an invisible altar.

No te bastaba
El sol de lengua ardiente sobre el negro diamante de tu piel,
A lo largo de tantas lentas mañanas, ganadas en ocio celeste,
Llenas de un áureo polen, igual que la corola de alguna
  flor feliz,
De reposo divino, divina indiferencia;
Caído el cuerpo flexible y seguro, como un arma mortal,
Ante la gran criatura enigmática, el mar inexpresable,
Sin deseo ni pena, igual a un dios,
Que sin embargo hubiera conocido, a semejanza del hombre,
Nuestros deseos estériles, nuestras penas perdidas.

Mira también hacia lo lejos
Aquellas oscuras tardes, cuando severas nubes,
Denso enjambre de negras alas,
Silencio y zozobra vertían sobre el mar;
Y en tanto las gaviotas encarnaban la angustia del aire invadido
  por la tormenta,
Recuérdale agitado, al mar, sacudiendo su entraña,
Como demente que quisiera arrancar en la luz
El núcleo secreto de su mal,
Torciendo en olas su pálido cuerpo,
Su inagotable cuerpo dolido,
Trastornado ante tu amor, también inagotable,
Sin que pudieras llevar sobre su frente atormentada
La concha protectora de una mano.

Las gracias vagabundas de abril
Abrieron sus menudas hojas sobre la arena perezosa.
Una juventud nueva corría por las venas de los hombres
  invernales;
Escapaban timideces, escalofríos, pudores
Ante el puñal radiante del deseo,
Palabra ensordecedora para la criatura dolida en cuerpo
  y espíritu

For you, the sun running its hot tongue
Over the dark diamond of your skin all through the length
Of so many slow mornings given to heavenly leisure,
Suffused with a golden pollen, like the corolla of some
   happy flower,
In divine repose, divine indifference,
Was not enough; your limber, agile body dropped like a
   deadly weapon
Into the great unknowable creature, the inexpressible ocean,
Neither suffering nor desiring, like some god
Who nonetheless might know in human form
Our barren desires, our lost sorrows.

And look far out
Into those dark afternoons when grave clouds,
Dense swarms of black wings,
Poured their rumbling silence into the sea;
Even the gulls thrashed by the storm embodied the air's anguish,
Remember the ocean's agitation shuddering from its depths
Like a madman trying to force up into the light
The hidden core of his illness,
Twisting its pale body into the shapes of waves,
Its inexhaustible aching body,
Writhing for your love, it too inexhaustible,
And you unable to raise even the shell of a hand
To shield your storm lashed face.

The vagabond graces of April
Unfurled their little leaves above the lazy sand.
A new youth started moving in the veins of wintery men;
Shyness, modesty, chills ran free
Before the gleaming dagger of desire,
A deafening word for one wounded body and soul

Por las terribles mordeduras del amor,
Porque el deseo se yergue sobre los despojos de la tormenta
Cuando arde el sol en las playas del mundo.

Mas ¿qué importan a mi vida las playas del mundo?
Es ésta solamente quien clava mi memoria,
Porque en ella te vi cruzar, sombrío como una negra aurora,
Arrastrando las alas de tu hermosura
Sobre su dilatada curva, semejante a una pomposa rama
Abierta bajo la luz,
Con su armadura de altas rocas
Caída hacia las dunas de adelfas y de palmas,
En lánguido paraje del perezoso sur.

Aún ven mis ojos las salinas de sonrosadas aguas,
Los leves molinos de viento
Y aquellos menudos cuerpos oscuros,
Parsimoniosamente movibles,
Junto a los bueyes fulvos,
Transportando los lunáticos bloques de sal
Sobre las vagonetas, tristes como todo lo que pertenece a los
trabajos de la tierra,
Hasta las anchas barcas resbaladizas sobre el pecho del mar.

Quién podría vivir en la tierra
Si no fuera por el mar.

Cuántas veces te vi,
Acariciados los ligeros tobillos por el ancho círculo de tu
pantalón marino,
El pecho y los hombros dilatados sobre la armoniosa cintura,
Cubierto voluptuosamente de lana azul como de yedra,
El desdén esculpido sobre los duros labios,
Anegarte frente al mar en una contemplación
Más honda que la del hombre frente al cuerpo que ama.

By the bites of love's terrifying teeth,
Because desire is erected on the storm's wrack
When the sun blazes on the world's beaches.

But what do I care about the world's beaches?
This beach is the only one nailed in my memory,
Because here's where I saw you walking, dark as a black dawn,
Dragging the wings of your beauty
Across its expansive curve, like a branch exploding with opening
Blossoms under the sunlight,
With its armor of tall cliffs
Fallen into its oleander and palm dotted dunes
In that languid place in the lazy south.

I can still see those rosy, salty swells,
The breeze's light mills
And those small dark bodies,
Just slightly moving,
Near the beasts of burden
Hauling the lunatic blocks of salt
Atop the wagons, sad like everything else connected with earthly
   labor,
Even the big boats sliding over the breast of the sea.

Who could live on earth
If not for the sea.

I saw you so many times,
Your delicate ankles caressed by the ample ring of your
   bellbottoms,
Your chest and shoulders spread above your slender waist,
Voluptuously draped in blue wool like ivy,
Indifference sculpted on your tough lips,
Immersed in contemplation gazing out to sea,
More mesmerized than a man by his lover's body.

Cambiantes sentimientos nos enlazan con este o aquel cuerpo,
Y todos ellos no son sino sombras que velan
La forma suprema del amor, que por sí mismo late,
Ciego ante las mudanzas de los cuerpos,
Iluminado por el ardor de su propia llama invencible.

Y te adoraba como cifra de todo cuerpo bello,
Sin velos que mudaran la recóndita imagen del amor;
Más que al mismo amor, más, ¿me oyes?,
Insaciable como tú mismo,
Inagotable como tú mismo;
Aun sabiendo que el mar era el único ser de la creación digno
de ti
Y tu cuerpo el único digno de su inhumana soberbia.

Era el atardecer. Las aves del día
Huyeron ante el furtivo pensamiento de la sombra.
Los hombres descansaban en sus cabañas,
Entre la mujer y los hijos,
Desnudos los pies bajo la luz funeral del acetileno,
Acechando el sueño en sus yacijas junto al mar;
Como si no pudieran dormir lejos de lo que les hace vivir
Y de lo que les hace morir.

Un gran silencio, una gran calma
Daba con su presencia el mar;
Pero también latía por el aire adormecido y fresco del
letal anochecer
Un miedo oscuro
A no se sabe qué pálidos gigantes,
Dueños de grisáceas serpientes y negros hipocampos,
Abriendo las sombrías aguas,
En lucha sus miembros retorcidos con rebeldes potencias
animales del abismo.

We are entangled in changing emotions with one or another
body,
And all of them no more than shadows obscuring
Love's supreme form, which throbs for itself,
Blind to the changing of bodies,
Lit by the heat of its own invincible flame.

I adored you as an emblem of every beautiful body,
Stripped of the veils that mask the hidden image of love;
More than love itself, more, do you hear me?
Insatiable like you,
Inexhaustible like you;
Knowing the ocean was the only thing in creation worthy of you
And your body the only one worthy of its inhuman
magnificence.

The sun was going down. The day's birds
Flew off before the furtive thoughts of the dark.
Men were lying in their bungalows
Beside their wives and children,
Barefoot in funereal artificial light,
Stalking dreams in their beachfront beds,
As if unable to sleep too far from what gives them life
And what brings them death.

The ocean's presence
Gave off a vast silence, a vast calm;
But also pulsing in the cool and sleepy air of that lethal sundown
Was a dark fear
Of who knows what pale monsters,
Masters of grayish serpents and black seahorses
Opening the murky waters,
Their twisted limbs wrestling with rebellious beastly powers of
the abyss.

Las barcas, como leves espectros,
Surgían lentamente desde la arena soñolienta,
Voluptuosos cuerpos tibios,
Con la gracia del animal que sabe volver los ojos implorantes
Hacia las manos de su dueño, dispensadoras de protección y de caricias,
Y piensa tristemente que se alejan sin poder retenerlas.

No a estas horas,
No a estas horas de tregua cobarde,
Al amanecer es cuando debías ir hacia el mar, joven marino,
Desnudo como una flor;
Y entonces es cuando debías amarle, cuando el mar debía poseerte,
Cuerpo a cuerpo,
Hasta confundir su vida con la tuya
Y despertar en ti su inmenso amor
El breve espasmo de tu placer sometido,
Desposados el uno con el otro,
Vida con vida, muerte con muerte.

Y una vez, como rosa dejada,
Flotó tu cuerpo, apenas deformado por las nupciales caricias del mar,
Mas pálidos los labios, lo mismo que si hubieran dado paso
A toda su pasión, el ave de la vida;
Igualmente hermoso así, joven marino,
Desgarradoramente triste con tu belleza inhabitada,
Como cuando tornasolaba la vida tus miembros melodiosos.

Cambian las vidas, pero la muerte es única.
Aún oigo aquella voz exangüe, que en su vago delirio
Llegó hasta mí, a través de las velas caídas en la arena, como alas arrancadas;

The ghostly specters of boats
Rose slowly out of the drowsy sand,
Voluptuous cool bodies
With the grace of an animal turning its gaze to implore
Its master, whose hands provide protection and caresses,
And sees them pulling away and knows it can never keep them.

Not at this hour,
Not at this hour of cowardly repose,
At dawn, young sailor, is when you had to go down to the ocean
Naked as a flower;
And that's when you had to give it your love, when the sea could
possess you,
Body to body,
Until its life and yours were mixed together
And its tremendous love awoke in you
The brief spasm of consummated pleasure,
Wedded one with the other,
Life with life, death with death.

And just that once, like a cut rose,
Your body floated scarcely deformed by the ocean's nuptial
caresses,
But your lips were a little pale, as if all your passion, the wings
of life,
Had flown out from between them;
You were equally beautiful that way, young man of the sea,
Painfully sad in your uninhabited beauty,
As when the life in your musical limbs was iridescent.

Lives change, but death is constant.
I can still hear that bloodless voice, which in its delirium
Reached me across the sails washed up on the beach like torn off
wings;

Alguien que conocía tu ausencia, porque sus ojos te vieron
muerto, tal una rosa abandonada sobre el mar
Decía lentamente: "Era más ligero que el agua."

Qué desiertos los hombres,
Cómo chocan sin verse unos a otros sus frentes de vergüenza,
Y cuán dulce será rodar, igual que tú, del otro lado, en
el olvido.
Así tu muerte despierta en mí el deseo de la muerte,
Como tu vida despertaba en mí el deseo de la vida.

Someone who understood you were gone, because he could see
you were dead,
Like a rose tossed into the sea, said slowly: "He was lighter
than water."

Men are so empty,
So full of shame they collide without seeing each other,
But how sweet it will be to roll, exactly like you, on the other
side, in oblivion.
That's how your death awakens in me the desire to die,
Just as your life awakened in me the desire to live.

HIMNO A LA TRISTEZA

Fortalecido estoy contra tu pecho
De augusta piedra fría,
Bajo tus ojos crepusculares,
Oh madre inmortal.

Desengañada alienta en ti mi vida,
Oyendo en el pausado retiro nocturno
Ligeramente resbalar las pisadas
De los días juveniles, que se alejan
Apacibles y graves, en la mirada,
Con una misma luz, compasión y reproche;
Y van tras ellos, como irisado humo,
Los sueños creados con mi pensamiento,
Los hijos del anhelo y la esperanza.

La soledad poblé de seres a mi imagen
Como un dios aburrido;
Los amé si eran bellos,
Mi compañía les di cuando me amaron,
Y ahora como ese mismo dios aislado estoy,
Inerme y blanco tal una flor cortada.

Olvidándome voy en este vago cuerpo,
Nutrido por las hierbas leves
Y las brillantes frutas de la tierra,
El pan y el vino alados,
En mi nocturno lecho a solas.

Hijo de tu leche sagrada,
El esbelto mancebo
Hiende con pie inconsciente
La escarpada colina,

Hymn to Sadness

Under your twilight eyes,
Close to your breast of cold, noble stone,
I am made strong,
Immortal mother.

With no illusions left my life is fed by you,
Those footsteps softly fading into the distance
Of the retreating night
Are the sounds of my youth gravely and gently
Slipping out of sight, with a glance
Full of light, compassion and reproach;
And in their wake, like rainbows of smoke,
The dreams my thought invented,
Children of hope and desire.

Like a bored god, I peopled my solitude
With creatures in my own image;
I loved them if they were lovely,
I went along with them when they loved me,
And now I'm just as abandoned as that god,
Defenseless, faded as a cut flower.

Alone in my bed all night,
I'm being forgotten in this fading body,
Fed on the light grasses
And shining fruits of the land,
The bread and wine with wings.

Child of your sacred milk,
The slim young man
Makes his way unaware
Up your steep slope,

Salvando con la mirada en ti
El laurel frágil y la espina insidiosa.

Al amante aligeras las atónitas horas
De su soledad, cuando en desierta estancia
La ventana, sobre apacible naturaleza,
Bajo una luz lejana,
Ante sus ojos nebulosos traza
Con renovado encanto verdeante
La estampa inconsciente de su dicha perdida.

Tú nos devuelves vírgenes las horas
Del pasado; fuertes bajo el hechizo
De tu mirada inmensa,
Como guerrero intacto
En su fuerza desnudo tras de broquel broncíneo,
Serenos vamos bajo los blancos arcos del futuro.

Ellos, los dioses, alguna vez olvidan
El tosco hilo de nuestros trabajados días,
Pero tú, celeste donadora recóndita,
Nunca los ojos quitas de tus hijos
Los hombres, por el mal hostigados.

Viven y mueren a solas los poetas,
Restituyendo en claras lágrimas
La polvorienta agua salobre,
Y en alta gloria resplandeciente
La esquiva ojeada del magnate henchido,
Mientras sus nombres suenan
Con el viento en las rocas,
Entre el hosco rumor de torrentes oscuros,
Allá por los espacios donde el hombre
Nunca puso sus plantas.

His eyes on you, gathering
Fragile laurels and hidden thorns.

You lighten the stunned hours of the lover's
Solitude, in some empty room
Whose window looks out on a calm landscape
Under a faraway moon;
Before his cloudy eyes you sketch
With refreshed enchantment
The green unconscious image of his lost happiness.

You give us back the hours of the past
Untouched; empowered by the spell
Of your vast gaze,
Like a warrior naked and strong
Behind his bronze shield,
We walk sure of ourselves through the future's white arches.

They, the gods, sometimes forget
The bitter hardness of our daily labors,
But you, sky hidden protector,
Never take your eyes off your human
Children, no matter how badly beaten.

Poets live and die all by themselves,
Distilling brackish water
Into clear tears,
And the sneering glance of the well fed big shot
Into a gleaming glory,
While the windswept rocks
Echo their names
Amid the harsh murmurs of the dark currents
Out there in the realm where people
Never set foot.

¿Quién sino tú caída sus vidas, les da fuerzas
Para alzar la mirada entre tanta miseria,
En la hermosura perdidos ciegamente?
¿Quién sino tú, amante y madre eterna?

Escucha cómo avanzan las generaciones
Sobre esta remota tierra misteriosa;
Marchan hostigados los hombres
Bajo la yerta sombra de los antepasados,
Y el cuerpo fatigado se reclina
Sobre la misma huella tibia
De otra carne precipitada en el olvido.

Luchan algunos por fijar nuestro anhelo,
Como si hubiera alguien, más fuerte que nosotros,
Que tuviera en memoria nuestro olvido;
Porque dulce será anegarse
En un abrazo inmenso,
Vuelto niebla con luz, agua en la tormenta;
Grato ha de ser aniquilarse,
Marchitas en los labios las delirantes voces.

Mas todavía hay en mí algo que te reclama
Conmigo hacia los parques de la muerte
Para acallar el miedo ante la sombra.
¿Dónde floreces tú, como vaga corola
Henchida del piadoso aroma que te alienta
En las nupcias terrenas con los hombres?
No eres hiel ni eres pena, sino amor de justicia imposible,
Tú, la compasión humana de los dioses.

Who except you watches over their lives, gives them the strength
To keep looking up amid so much misery,
Blindly lost in beauty as they are.
Who except you, eternal mother, lover.

Listen to the generations as they advance
Across this immense mysterious earth;
See men marching under the lash
Of their ancestors' rigid shadows,
Tired flesh inclined
Down the same halfbaked track
Of another body flung into oblivion.

Some of us try to affix our desire,
As if there were someone stronger than we are
Who could remember our forgottenness;
Because it will be sweet to disappear
Into some great embrace
And be turned into shining fog, storm tossed water;
A pleasure to be annihilated,
Our delirious voices withering on our lips.

But something in me still needs you here
Beside me heading for the parks of death
To calm my fears as I face the dark.
Where do you bloom, like some strange flower
Filled with the merciful scent you breathe
In the bridal bed of humanity?
You are neither bitterness nor sorrow,
But love for a justice that will never be,
You, human compassion of the gods.

A LAS ESTATUAS DE LOS DIOSES

Hermosas y vencidas soñáis,
Vueltos los ciegos ojos hacia el cielo,
Mirando las remotas edades
De titánicos hombres,
Cuyo amor os daba ligeras guirnaldas
Y la olorosa llama se alzaba
Hacia la luz divina, su hermana celeste.

Reflejo de vuestra verdad, las criaturas
Adictas y libres como el agua iban;
Aún no había mordido la brillante maldad
Sus cuerpos llenos de majestad y gracia.
En vosotros creían y vosotros existíais;
La vida no era un delirio sombrío.

La miseria y la muerte futuras,
No pensadas aún, en vuestras manos
Bajo un inofensivo sueño adormecían
Sus venenosas flores bellas,
Y una y otra vez el mismo amor tornaba
Al pecho de los hombres,
Como ave fiel que vuelve al nido
Cuando el día, entre las altas ramas,
Con apacible risa va entornando los ojos.

Eran tiempos heroicos y frágiles,
Deshechos con vuestro poder como un sueño feliz.
Hoy yacéis, mutiladas y oscuras,
Entre los grises jardines de las ciudades,
Piedra inútil que el soplo celeste no anima,
Abandonadas de la súplica y la humana esperanza.

To the Statues of the Gods

Beautiful and defeated,
Eyes cast heavenward
Gazing at the faraway ages,
You dream of titanic men
Whose love gave you delicate garlands
And their fragrant flame was raised
Toward the sacred light, your celestial sister.

Reflecting your truth, your human
Adherents flowed along free as water,
Their bodies full of grace and majesty
As yet unwounded by blinding evil.
They believed in you and you existed;
Life was not a dark delirium.

As yet unimagined, death and misery
To come were half asleep, their beautiful
Poisonous blossoms under a harmless spell
In your hands,
And time and again love returned
To men's hearts
Like a faithful bird to the nest
When daylight, up in the high branches,
Crinkled their eyes with gentle laughter.

Those were fragile and heroic times,
Undone with your power like a sweet dream.
Now you lie unknown and mutilated
In the gray gardens of cities,
Useless stone unmoved by heavenly breezes,
Abandoned by human hopes and supplications.

La lluvia con la luz resbalan
Sobre tanta muerte memorable,
Mientras desfilan a lo lejos muchedumbres
Que antaño impíamente desertaron
Vuestros marmóreos altares,
Santificados en la memoria del poeta.

Tal vez su fe os devuelva el cielo.
Mas no juzguéis por el rayo, la guerra o la plaga
Una triste humanidad decaída;
Impasibles reinad en el divino espacio.
Distraiga con su gracia el copero solícito
La cólera de vuestro poder que despierta.

En tanto el poeta, en la noche otoñal,
Bajo el blanco embeleso lunático,
Mira las ramas que el verdor abandona
Nevarse de luz beatamente,
Y sueña con vuestro trono de oro
Y vuestra faz cegadora,
Lejos de los hombres,
Allá en la altura impenetrable.

The rain gleams as it slides down
So much memorable death,
While in the distance march the multitudes
Who long ago deserted
Your marble altars
Sanctified in poets' memory.

Perhaps heaven will return their faith to you.
But don't judge lowly, sad humanity
With lightning, wars or plagues;
Rule at ease from a serene height.
Allow this humble cup bearer to distract you
From the awakening fury of your power.

As for the poet, on this autumn night
Under the white spell of moonlight,
He looks up at trees shedding their leaves,
Branches blessed with snowy radiance,
And dreams of your golden thrones
And your dazzling faces
So far from men,
Up there in the impenetrable heights.

from

Las Nubes
Clouds
[1937–1940]

NOCHE DE LUNA

Vida tras vida, fueron
Olvidando los hombres
Aquella diosa virgen
Que misteriosamente, desde el cielo,
Con amor apacible
Asiste a sus vigilias
En el silencio dulce de las noches.

Ella ha sido quien viera a los abuelos
Remotos, cuando abordan
En sus pintados barcos,
Y ágiles y desnudos se apoderan
Con un trémulo imperio de esta tierra
Así como el amante
Arrebata y penetra el cuerpo amado.

Sus trabajos vio luego, sus cohabitaciones,
Y otros seres menudos,
Inhábiles, gritando entre los brazos
De los dominadores, y sus mujeres lánguidas
Sonreír débilmente a la raza naciente.

Miró sus largas guerras
Con pueblos enemigos
Y el azote sagrado
De luchas fratricidas;
Contempló esclavitudes y triunfos,
Prostituciones, crímenes,
Prosperidad, traiciones,
El sordo griterío,
Todo el horror humano que salva la hermosura,
Y con ella la calma,
La paz donde brota la historia.

Full Moon Night

Life after life, humanity
Went on forgetting
That virgin goddess
Who from the sky mysteriously
With gentle love
Keeps constant watch
In night's sweet silences.

She was the one who saw the far off
Ancestors boarding
Their painted boats,
Athletically taking over the earth
With trembling arrogance,
The way a seducer
Subdues and invades his lover's body.

Then she witnessed their works, their housekeeping,
And the little babies,
Helpless, crying in the arms
Of the conquerors, and their languid women
Smiling weakly over the newborn race.

She watched their endless wars
Against enemy tribes
And the sacred lashings
Of fratricidal struggles;
She gazed on slaveries and victories,
Prostitutions, crimes,
Prosperity, betrayals,
The deafening screams,
All the human horror redeemed by beauty,
And with beauty comes the calm,
The peace that gives rise to history.

También miró el arado
Con el siervo pasando
Sobre el antiguo campo de batalla,
Fertilizado por tanto cuerpo joven;
Y en ese mismo suelo ha visto correr luego
Al orgulloso dueño sobre caballos recios,
Mientras la hierba, ortiga y cardo
Brotaban por las vastas propiedades.

Cuánta sangre ha corrido
Ante el destino intacto de la diosa.
Cuánto semen viril
Vio surgir entre espasmos
De cuerpos hoy deshechos
En el viento y el polvo,
Cuyos átomos yerran en leves nubes grises,
Velando al embeleso de vasta descendencia
Su tranquilo semblante compasivo.

Cuántas claras ruinas,
Con jaramago apenas adornadas,
Como fuertes castillos un día las ha visto;
Piedras más elocuentes que los siglos,
Antes holladas por el paso leve
De esbeltas cazadoras, un neblí sobre el puño,
Oblicua la mirada soñolienta
Entre un aburrimiento y un amor clandestino.

Sombras, sombras efímeras,
En tanto ella, adolescente
Como en los prados de la edad de oro,
Vierte, azulada urna,
Su embeleso letal
Sobre nuevos cuerpos oscuros
Que la primavera enfebrece
Con agudos perfumes vegetales.

She also watched the slaves
Driving their plows
Over the old battlefields
Fertilized with the bodies of the young;
And then saw the landowners proudly riding
Their rugged horses over those lands
While grasses, nettles and spiky weeds
Sprang from the soil as far as the eye could see.

What seas of blood have flowed
Under the virgin gaze of the goddess.
What rivers of semen
She's witnessed surging in spasms
Between bodies now reduced
To dust in the wind,
Their atoms now scattered in wispy clouds,
Her sympathetic face
Calmly observing the raptures of generations.

How many moonlit ruins
With weeds now springing up between the stones
She once looked on as mighty castles;
Stones more eloquent than the centuries,
Once grazed by the light footsteps
Of slender huntresses, falcons on their fists,
Their sleepy gaze averted
Between boredom and some clandestine love affair.

Shadows, passing shadows,
While she, still young
As she was above the plains of the Golden Age,
Still pours from her blue pitcher
A lethal potion
Over new dark bodies
Made feverish by spring
With its sharp, sweet, flowery scents.

Allá tras de las torres, su reflejo
Delata la presencia del mar,
Mientras los hombres solitarios duermen
Inermes en su lecho y confiados.
Los enemigos yacen confundidos.
Algo inmenso reposa, aunque la muerte aceche.
Y el mágico reflejo entre los árboles
Permite al soñador abandonarse al canto,
Al placer y al reposo,
A lo que siendo efímero se sueña como eterno.

Mas una noche, al contemplar la antigua
Morada de los hombres, sólo ha de ver allá
Ese reflejo de su dulce fulgor,
Mudo y vacío entonces,
Estéril tal su hermosura virginal;
Sin que ningunos ojos humanos
Hasta ella se alcen a través de las lágrimas,
Definitivamente frente a frente
El silencio de un mundo que ha sido
Y la pura belleza tranquila de la nada.

Out beyond the towers, her reflection
Betrays the presence of the sea,
While solitary men lie fast asleep
Trusting and defenseless in their beds.
Enemies lie down and can't be told apart.
Something vast is at rest, though death is stalking.
And the magical reflection through the trees
Enables dreamers to give themselves to song,
To pleasure and repose,
To the ephemeral dreamed as if eternal.

But some night, looking down
On mankind's ancient home, all she'll see
Is that reflection of her own sweet shining,
Quietly empty then,
Barren as her virgin beauty;
With no more human eyes
Looking up at her through their tears,
Finally face to face
With the dead silence of a world that was
And the pure still beauty of nothingness.

A UN POETA MUERTO

(F. G. L.)

Así como en la roca nunca vemos
La clara flor abrirse,
Entre un pueblo hosco y duro
No brilla hermosamente
El fresco y alto ornato de la vida.
Por esto te mataron, porque eras
Verdor en nuestra tierra árida
Y azul en nuestro oscuro aire.

Leve es la parte de la vida
Que como dioses rescatan los poetas.
El odio y destrucción perduran siempre
Sordamente en la entraña
Toda hiel sempiterna del español terrible,
Que acecha lo cimero
Con su piedra en la mano.

Triste sino nacer
Con algún don ilustre
Aquí, donde los hombres
En su miseria sólo saben
El insulto, la mofa, el recelo profundo
Ante aquel que ilumina las palabras opacas
Por el oculto fuego originario.

La sal de nuestro mundo eras,
Vivo estabas como un rayo de sol,
Y ya es tan sólo tu recuerdo
Quien yerra y pasa, acariciando
El muro de los cuerpos

To a Dead Poet

(F. G. L.)

The same way we never see a bright flower
Blooming on rocky ground,
Out of a hard and sullen people
No shining jewel of life
Can beam its beauty.
That's why they killed you, because you were
A flash of green in our barren land
And blue in our blackened sky.

Lightness is the part of life
The poets save like gods.
Hatred and destruction go on forever
Deaf and dumb in the eternally bitter
Depths of the terrible Spaniard,
Who lies in wait for what's best
Clutching his rock.

It's a sad fate to be born
With some brilliant gift
Here, where men
In their misery know only
Insult, mockery, deep distrust
Of one who brightens dull words
With mysterious original fire.

You were the seasoning of our world,
Alive you were like a sunbeam,
And now it's only your memory
Wandering through here, caressing
The wall of bodies

Con el dejo de las adormideras
Que nuestros predecesores ingirieron
A orillas del olvido.

Si tu ángel acude a la memoria,
Sombras son estos hombres
Que aún palpitan tras las malezas de la tierra;
La muerte se diría
Más viva que la vida
Porque tú estás con ella,
Pasado el arco de su vasto imperio,
Poblándola de pájaros y hojas
Con tu gracia y tu juventud incomparables.

Aquí la primavera luce ahora.
Mira los radiantes mancebos
Que vivo tanto amaste
Efímeros pasar juntos al fulgor del mar.
Desnudos cuerpos bellos que se llevan
Tras de sí los deseos
Con su exquisita forma, y sólo encierran
Amargo zumo, que no alberga su espíritu
Un destello de amor ni de alto pensamiento.

Igual todo prosigue,
Como entonces, tan mágico,
Que parece imposible
La sombra en que has caído.
Mas un inmenso afán oculto advierte
Que su ignoto aguijón tan sólo puede
Aplacarse en nosotros con la muerte,
Como el afán del agua,
A quien no basta esculpirse en las olas,
Sino perderse anónima
En los limbos del mar.

With what's left of the opium poppies
Our ancestors planted
Along the edges of oblivion.

When your angel enters our memory,
Those men whose hearts still beat across the badlands
Of the earth are merely shadows;
It could be said that death
Is more alive than life
Because you're there,
Passed through the arch of its immense empire,
Your grace, your youth, your uniqueness
Filling it with leaves and birdsong.

Here spring is shining its light.
Look at the glowing boys
You loved so much in life
Passing in a flash by the blazing sea.
Beautiful naked bodies trailing
Desires behind them
With their exquisite shapes, and full of such
Bitter juice, since their spirits are missing
The gleam of love or brilliance of bright thought.

Everything goes on the same
As before, so full of magic
That the darkness you've fallen into
Seems impossible.
Yet some enormous buried passion warns
That its unknowable wound in us can be soothed
Only by death,
Like water's passion,
Which can't be sculpted in waves,
But must be lost and nameless
In the ocean's nowhere.

Pero antes no sabías
La realidad más honda de este mundo:
El odio, el triste odio de los hombres,
Que en ti señalar quiso
Por el acero horrible su victoria,
Con tu angustia postrera
Bajo la luz tranquila de Granada,
Distante entre cipreses y laureles,
Y entre tus propias gentes
Y por las mismas manos
Que un día servilmente te halagaran.

Para el poeta la muerte es la victoria;
Un viento demoníaco le impulsa por la vida,
Y si una fuerza ciega
Sin comprensión de amor
Transforma por un crimen
A ti, cantor, en héroe,
Contempla en cambio, hermano,
Cómo entre la tristeza y el desdén
Un poder más magnánimo permite a tus amigos
En un rincón pudrirse libremente.

Tenga tu sombra paz,
Busque otros valles,
Un río donde el viento
Se lleve los sonidos entre juncos
Y lirios y el encanto
Tan viejo de las aguas elocuentes,
En donde el eco como la gloria humana ruede,
Como ella de remoto,
Ajeno como ella y tan estéril.

Halle tu gran afán enajenado
El puro amor de un dios adolescente
Entre el verdor de las rosas eternas;

But then you never knew
The deepest truth in the world:
Hatred, men's sorry hatred,
That tried, with its terrible blade, to carve
Its victory in you,
With your final anguish
Under the peaceful sunlight of Granada,
Far off among laurels and cypresses,
And among your own people
And by the same hands
That someday will praise you with their lowly honors.

For a poet, death is victory;
A demonic wind sweeps him through life,
And if a blind force
That knows nothing of love
Can turn, with one crime,
A singer like you into a hero,
Consider, brother, on the other hand,
How between sadness and contempt
An even more generous power allows your friends
To go on rotting freely in some corner.

May your shade find peace,
And search for other valleys,
Some river where the wind
Plays sounds in its reeds
And the lilies and the age old spell
Of eloquent waters
Where an echo of human glory rolls on
Like the one long ago,
Equally alien, equally barren.

May your grand scorned passion find
The pure love of an adolescent god
There in a garden of eternal roses;

Porque este ansia divina, perdida aquí en la tierra,
Tras de tanto dolor y dejamiento,
Con su propia grandeza nos advierte
De alguna mente creadora inmensa,
Que concibe al poeta cual lengua de su gloria
Y luego le consuela a través de la muerte.

Because that divine longing, lost here on earth
After so much pain and loss,
With its own greatness shows us
There is some vast mind of creation
That conceives a poet whose language is his glory
And then consoles him after he is gone.

Translator's note: Federico García Lorca, a friend of Cernuda, was murdered by fascist forces in 1936 in the first days of the Spanish Civil War.

ELEGÍA ESPAÑOLA [I]

Dime, háblame
Tú, esencia misteriosa
De nuestra raza
Tras de tantos siglos,
Hálito creador
De los hombres hoy vivos,
A quienes veo por el odio impulsados
Hasta ofrecer sus almas
A la muerte, la patria más profunda.

Cuando la primavera vieja
Vuelva a tejer su encanto
Sobre tu cuerpo inmenso,
¿Cuál ave hallará nido
Y qué savia una rama
Donde brotar con verde impulso?
¿Qué rayo de la luz alegre,
Qué nube sobre el campo solitario,
Hallarán agua, cristal de hogar en calma
Donde reflejen su irisado juego?

Háblame, madre;
Y al llamarte así, digo
Que ninguna mujer lo fue de nadie
Como tú lo eres mía.
Háblame, dime
Una sola palabra en estos días lentos,
En los días informes
Que frente a ti se esgrimen
Como cuchillo amargo
Entre las manos de tus propios hijos.

Elegy for Spain [I]

Tell me, speak to me,
Mysterious essence
Of our blood streaming
Through so many centuries,
Animating spirit
Of men now living
Visibly driven by hatred
To offer their souls
To death, the most fathomless country of all.

When old springtime
Returns to weave its spell
Over your vast body,
What bird will find a nest
And what sap a branch
To pump its green pulse through?
What beam of happy light,
What cloud over the lonely landscape
Will find water or the window of a calm home
To reflect its playful rainbows?

Speak to me, Mother;
And by that I mean
No woman was ever to anyone
What you are to me.
Speak to me, tell me
A single word in these long days,
These chaotic days
Dueling before you
Like bitter knives
In the hands of your own children.

No te alejes así, ensimismada
Bajo los largos velos cenicientos
Que nos niegan tus anchos ojos bellos.
Esas flores caídas,
Pétalos rotos entre sangre y lodo,
En tus manos estaban luciendo eternamente
Desde siglos atrás, cuando mi vida
Era un sueño en la mente de los dioses.

Eres tú, son tus ojos lo que busca
Quien te llama luchando con la muerte,
A ti, remota y enigmática
Madre de tantas almas idas
Que te legaron, con un fulgor de piedra clara,
Su afán de eternidad cifrado en hermosura.

Pero no eres tan sólo
Dueña de afanes muertos;
Tierna, amorosa has sido con nuestro afán viviente,
Compasiva con nuestra desdicha de efímeros.
¿Supiste acaso si de ti éramos dignos?

Contempla ahora a través de las lágrimas:
Mira cuántos traidores,
Mira cuántos cobardes
Lejos de ti en fuga vergonzosa,
Renegando tu nombre y tu regazo,
Cuando a tus pies, mientras la larga espera,
Si desde el suelo alzamos hacia ti la mirada,
Tus hijos sienten oscuramente
La recompensa de estas horas fatídicas.

No sabe qué es la vida
Quien jamás alentó bajo la guerra.
Ella sobre nosotros sus alas densas cierne,
Y oigo su silbo helado,

Don't drift off, lost in yourself
Under those big gray sails
Hiding from us your beautiful wide eyes.
Those fallen flowers,
Their petals crushed in the mud and the blood,
Shone eternally in your hands
For centuries, ever since my life
Was no more than a dream in the mind of the gods.

It's you, it's your eyes I'm looking for,
Calling out to you in your struggle with death,
You, remote and inscrutable
Mother of so many vanished souls
Who left you, in the bright glow of your stone,
Their passion for eternity fixed in beauty.

But you are not only
Guardian of dead passions;
You've been tender and loving with our living one,
Compassionate toward our misfortune of being transient.
Did you really consider us worthy of you?

Now through your tears consider
How many traitors,
How many cowards
Shamelessly deserted you
Renouncing your name and your comfort,
While at your feet, all through the long wait,
If we look up from the dirt to gaze at you,
Your children vaguely have some sense
Of compensation for these dreadful times.

No one who hasn't breathed the stench of war
Knows what life is.
It spreads its thick wings over us
And I hear its icy shriek

Y veo los muertos bruscos
Caer sobre la hierba calcinada,
Mientras el cuerpo mío
Sufre y lucha con unos enfrente de esos otros.

No sé qué tiembla y muere en mí
Al verte así dolida y solitaria,
En ruinas los claros dones
De tus hijos, a través de los siglos;
Porque mucho he amado tu pasado,
Resplandor victorioso entre sombra y olvido.

Tu pasado eres tú
Y al mismo tiempo eres
La aurora que aún no alumbra nuestros campos.
Tú sola sobrevives
Aunque venga la muerte;
Sólo en ti está la fuerza
De hacernos esperar a ciegas el futuro.

Que por encima de estos y esos muertos
Y encima de estos y esos vivos que combaten,
Algo advierte que tú sufres con todos.
Y su odio, su crueldad, su lucha,
Ante ti vanos son, como sus vidas,
Porque tú eres eterna
Y sólo los creaste
Para la paz y gloria de su estirpe.

And I see its suddenly dead
Falling into the bleached grass
While my own body
Suffers and struggles with one side against the other.

I can't tell what's trembling and dying in me
To see you so wounded and alone,
The bright gifts of your children
In ruins after so many centuries;
Because I've loved your past so much,
Its undefeated gleam between darkness and nothingness.

You are your past
And at the same time you are
The sunrise yet to come up over our fields.
Only you will survive
Though death may also come;
Only in you is the strength
To keep us blindly hoping for the future.

Because over and above all these deaths
And over and above all those alive and fighting,
Something tells me you are suffering too,
And their hatreds, their cruelties, their battles
Are nothing to you, like their lives,
Because you are eternal
And created them only
For peace and for the glory of their successors.

SOÑANDO LA MUERTE

Como una blanca rosa
Cuyo halo en lo oscuro los ojos no perciben;
Como un blanco deseo
Que ante el amor caído invisible se alzara;
Como una blanca llama
Que en aire torna siempre la mentira del cuerpo,
Por el día solitario y la noche callada
Pasas tú, sombra eterna,
Con un dedo en los labios.

Vas en la blanca nube que orlándose de fuego
De un dios es ya el ala transparente;
En la blanca ladera, por el valle
Donde velan, verdes lebreles místicos, los chopos;
En la blanca figura de los hombres,
De vivir olvidados con su sueño y locura;
En todo pasas tú, sombra enigmática,
Y quedamente suenas
Tal un agua a esta fiebre de la vida.

Cuando la blanca juventud miro caída,
Manchada y rota entre las grises horas;
Cuando la blanca verdad veo traicionada
Por manos ambiciosas y bocas elocuentes;
Cuando la blanca inspiración siento perdida
Ante los duros siglos en el dolor pasados,
Sólo en ti creo entonces, vasta sombra,
Tras los sombríos mirtos de tu pórtico
Única realidad clara del mundo.

Dreaming of Death

Like a white rose
Whose halo is invisible in the dark;
Like a white desire
Fallen for love and invisibly rising;
Like a white flame
Forever revealing the body as a lie,
Through solitary days and silent nights
You move, eternal shadow,
With a finger at your lips.

You float in white clouds, transparent wings
Edged with the fire of some god;
And fill white hillsides and valleys where poplars,
Those green mystical greyhounds, still keep watch;
And live in the white shapes of men
Forgotten with their dreams and madnesses;
You move through everything, mysterious shadow,
And you sound steadily
Like water flowing through this feverish life.

When I see white youth gone down
Stained and broken in the gray hours;
When I see white truth betrayed
By ambitious hands and eloquent mouths;
When I feel white inspiration lost
Before the hard sufferings of centuries past,
Then I believe in you alone, vast shadow,
And through the dark myrtles of your portico
Can see the one clear reality of the world.

A LARRA CON UNAS VIOLETAS
[1837–1937]

Aún se queja su alma vagamente,
El oscuro vacío de su vida.
Mas no pueden pesar sobre esa sombra
Algunas violetas,
Y es grato así dejarlas
Frescas entre la niebla,
Con la alegría de una menuda cosa pura
Que rescatara aquel dolor antiguo.

Quien habla ya a los muertos,
Mudo le hallan los que viven.
Y en este otro silencio, donde el miedo impera,
Recoger esas flores una a una
Breve consuelo ha sido entre los días
Cuya huella sangrienta llevan las espaldas
Por el odio cargadas con una piedra inútil.

Si la muerte apacigua
Tu boca amarga de Dios insatisfecha,
Acepta un don tan leve, sombra sentimental,
En esa paz que bajo tierra te esperaba,
Brotando en hierba, viento y luz silvestres,
El fiel y último encanto de estar solo.

Curado de la vida, por una vez sonríe,
Pálido rostro de pasión y de hastío.
Mira las calles viejas por donde fuiste errante,
El farol azulado que te guiara, carne yerta,
Al regresar del baile o del sucio periódico,
Y las fuentes de mármol entre palmas:
Aguas y hojas, bálsamo del triste.

For Larra with a Few Violets
[1837–1937]

His soul still vaguely complains
About the empty darkness where it's living.
But a few violets won't weigh much
On that shade,
And it feels good to leave them,
Fresh in the gray fog,
With the joy of a small pure thing
That might relieve some of that old pain.

Whoever speaks with the dead
The living perceive as silent.
And in this other silence ruled by fear,
Gathering these flowers one by one
Has been some consolation in these days
Where we leave such bloody tracks shouldering our loads
Of useless rock through a landscape of hate.

If death has calmed
Your bitter mouth of an irritable God,
Accept such a light gift, a shadow of my feelings,
In that peace that received you into the earth,
Sprouting in grass, a breeze and idyllic light
The faithful and final enchantment of being left alone.

Cured of life, for once your pale, passionate,
Disgusted face can smile.
Look at the old streets where you once wandered,
The blue flame of the streetlamps that guided you, stiff corpse,
On the way home from the dance or the inky newspaper,
And the marble fountains amid the palms:
Water and leaves, balm for the sad man.

La tierra ha sido medida por los hombres,
Con sus casas estrechas y matrimonios sórdidos,
Su venenosa opinión pública y sus revoluciones
Más crueles e injustas que las leyes,
Como inmenso bostezo demoníaco;
No hay sitio en ella para el hombre solo,
Hijo desnudo y deslumbrante del divino pensamiento.

Y nuestra gran madrastra, mírala hoy deshecha,
Miserable y aún bella entre las tumbas grises
De los que como tú, nacidos en su estepa,
Vieron mientras vivían morirse la esperanza,
Y gritaron entonces, sumidos por tinieblas,
A hermanos irrisorios que jamás escucharon.

Escribir en España no es llorar, es morir,
Porque muere la inspiración envuelta en humo,
Cuando no va su llama libre en pos del aire.
Así, cuando el amor, el tierno monstruo rubio,
Volvió contra ti mismo tantas ternuras vanas,
Tu mano abrió de un tiro, roja y vasta, la muerte.

Libre y tranquilo quedaste en fin un día,
Aunque tu voz sin ti abrió un dejo indeleble.
Es breve la palabra como el canto de un pájaro,
Mas un claro jirón puede prenderse en ella
De embriaguez, pasión, belleza fugitivas,
Y subir, ángel vigía que atestigua del hombre,
Allá hasta la región celeste e impasible.

Earth has been caught and measured by men
With their narrow houses and sordid marriages,
Their poisonous public opinion and their revolutions
Even more cruel and unjust than their laws,
Like some demonic yawn that swallows everyone;
There's no place on it for the individual,
Naked shining child of divine thought.

And our great stepmother, look how undone she is,
Miserable yet still lovely among the gray tombs
Of those who, like you, born on her plain,
Saw during their lives the death of hope
And cried out, overcome by darkness,
To ridiculous brothers who never listened.

To write in Spain is not to cry but to die,
Because inspiration dies when cloaked in smoke,
When its flame can't burn freely in the air.
And so, when love, that sweet blond monster,
Turned against you so many vain affections,
Your hand, with one thunderous red shot, broke death open.

So one day you finally found freedom and peace,
Though your voice without you left an indelible trace.
The word is brief as birdsong,
But a bright bit of drunkenness, passion, fleeting
Beauty can take it and soar,
A guardian angel that testifies for man,
Up there in that heavenly, inaccessible space.

Translator's note: Mariano José de Larra (1809–1837), one of Spain's great satirists and social critics, took his own life after several disappointments in love.

ELEGÍA ESPAÑOLA [II]

A Vicente Aleixandre

Ya la distancia entre los dos abierta
Se lleva el sufrimiento, como nube
Rota en lluvia olvidada, y la alegría,
Hermosa claridad desvanecida;
Nada altera entre tú, mi tierra, y yo,
Pobre palabra tuya, el invisible
Fluir de los recuerdos, sustentando
Almas con la verdad de tu alma pura.
Sin luchar contra ti ya asisto inerte
A la discordia estéril que te cubre,
Al viento de locura que te arrastra.
Tan sólo Dios vela sobre nosotros,
Árbitro inmemorial del odio eterno.

Tus pueblos han ardido y tus campos
Infecundos dan cosecha de hambre;
Rasga tu aire el ala de la muerte;
Tronchados como flores caen tus hombres
Hechos para el amor y la tarea;
Y aquellos que en la sombra suscitaron
La guerra, resguardados en la sombra,
Disfrutan su victoria. Tú en silencio,
Tierra, pasión única mía, lloras
Tu soledad, tu pena y tu vergüenza.

Fiel aún, extasiado como el pájaro
Que en primavera hacia su nido antiguo
Llegaba a ti y en ti dejaba el vuelo,
Con la atracción remota de un encanto
Ineludible, rosa del destino,
Mi espíritu se aleja de estas nieblas,
Canta su queja por tu cielo vasto,

Elegy for Spain [II]

for Vicente Aleixandre

Now the distance opened between us
Is swept away by suffering, like a cloud
Broken into long lost rain, and joy,
Its beautiful brightness scattered;
Nothing has changed between you, my land, and me,
Poor word of yours, the invisible
Stream of memories, sustaining
Souls with the truth of your pure soul.
Without fighting with you I witness helplessly
The sterile discord that covers you,
The wind of madness raking you.
God alone watches over us,
Immemorial arbiter of eternal hatred.

Your towns have burned and your barren
Fields yield a harvest of hunger;
Death's wing scrapes your skies;
People fall cut down like flowers,
Men and women made for work and love;
And the ones who in the shadows promoted
War, still crouching in the dark,
Savor their victory. You, in silence,
My land, my only passion, weep
Your solitude, your grief and your shame.

Still faithful, ecstatic like a bird
Who every spring returned to its nest
In you and settled
With the homing instinct of an inevitable
Spell, destiny's compass,
My spirit flies away from this fog,
Sings its complaint across your vast skies

Mientras el cuerpo queda vacilante,
Perdido, lejos, entre sueño y vida,
Y oye el susurro lento de las horas.

Si nunca más pudieran estos ojos
Enamorados reflejar tu imagen.
Si nunca más pudiera por tus bosques,
El alma en paz caída en tu regazo,
Soñar el mundo aquel que yo pensaba
Cuando la triste juventud lo quiso.
Tú nada más, fuerte torre en ruinas,
Puedes poblar mi soledad humana,
Y esta ausencia de todo en ti se duerme.
Deja tu aire ir sobre mi frente,
Tu luz sobre mi pecho hasta la muerte,
Única gloria cierta que aún deseo.

While my body remains uncertain,
Lost, far away, between life and sleep,
And can hear the slow rustling of the hours.

What if these loving eyes could never again
Reflect your image.
What if my soul could never again
Lie down to nap in the lap of your forests,
To dream that world I imagined
When my sad youth loved it.
You and you alone, strong tower in ruins,
Can fill my human solitude,
And this absolute absence rests in you.
Let your breezes blow across my face,
Your sun shine over my heart until I die,
The only certain glory I still desire.

NIÑO MUERTO

Si llegara hasta ti bajo la hierba
Joven como tu cuerpo, ya cubriendo
Un destierro más vasto con la muerte,
De los amigos la voz fugaz y clara,
Con oscura nostalgia quizá pienses
Que tu vida es materia del olvido.

Recordarás acaso nuestros días,
Este dejarse ir en la corriente
Insensible de trabajos y penas,
Este apagarse lento, melancólico,
Como las llamas de tu hogar antiguo,
Como la lluvia sobre aquel tejado.

Tal vez busques el campo de tu aldea,
El galopar alegre de los potros,
La amarillenta luz sobre las tapias,
La vieja torre gris, un lado en sombra,
Tal una mano fiel que te guiara
Por las sendas perdidas de la noche.

Recordarás cruzando el mar un día
Tu leve juventud con tus amigos
En flor, así alejados de la guerra.
La angustia resbalaba entre vosotros
Y el mar sombrío al veros sonreía,
Olvidando que él mismo te llevaba
A la muerte tras de un corto destierro.

Yo hubiera compartido aquellas horas
Yertas de un hospital. Tus ojos solos
Frente a la imagen dura de la muerte.

Dead Boy

If the bright, fleeting voices of your friends
Could reach you beneath the grass
Young as your body, already covering
An exile even more vast in death,
With a vague nostalgia you might think
Your life is the stuff of oblivion.

Maybe you recall our days together,
Letting ourselves be carried along on the current
With no idea of work or any sorrows,
That slow, melancholy fading away,
Like the fire going out in your old fireplace,
Like the sound of the rain on that rooftop.

Possibly now you're looking for your landscape,
The happy galloping of the young colts,
The yellow light along the top of the patio walls,
The old gray tower, one side in shadow,
Like a faithful hand that could be your guide
Along the night's lost pathways.

Maybe you remember your light youth
And that of your friends in flower one day
Crossing the ocean away from war.
Anguish slipped from one of you to another
And the dark ocean looked at you and smiled,
Unaware that it would carry you,
After a brief exile, to your death.

I would have loved to share those hours with you
When you were stiffening in a hospital bed.
Your eyes alone with the hard image of death.

Ese sueño de Dios no lo aceptaste.
Así como tu cuerpo era de frágil,
Enérgica y viril era tu alma.

De un solo trago largo consumiste
La muerte tuya, la que te destinaban,
Sin volver un instante la mirada
Atrás, igual que el hombre cuando lucha.
Inmensa indiferencia te cubría
Antes de que la tierra te cubriera.

El llanto que tú mismo no has llorado,
Yo lo lloro por ti. En mí no estaba
El ahuyentar tu muerte como a un perro
Enojoso. E inútil es que quiera
Ver tu cuerpo crecido, verde y puro,
Pasando como pasan estos otros
De tus amigos, por el aire blanco
De los campos ingleses, vivamente.

Volviste la cabeza contra el muro
Con el gesto de un niño que temiese
Mostrar fragilidad en su deseo.
Y te cubrió la eterna sombra larga.
Profundamente duermes. Mas escucha:
Yo quiero estar contigo; no estás solo.

That dream of God's was something you didn't accept.
Just as your body at the time was fragile,
Your soul was full of energy and virile.

In one long swallow you drank
Down your death, the one you were destined for,
Not looking back,
Like a man in battle.
Immense indifference covered you
Before the earth ever would.

The lament you never cried for yourself
I'm crying for you. Your death like a mad dog
Hunted down was not in me.
And my wanting to see your mature body,
Green and pure, wandering fully alive
Through the white air of the English countryside,
The same as these other friends of yours,
Is useless.

You turned your head to the wall
With the gesture of a child afraid
To reveal how fragile was his desire.
And eternity's long shadow came over you.
You are asleep at a great depth. But listen:
I want to be with you; you're not alone.

LA VISITA DE DIOS

Pasada se halla ahora la mitad de mi vida.
El cuerpo sigue en pie y las voces aún giran
Y resuenan con encanto marchito en mis oídos,
Mas los días esbeltos ya se marcharon lejos;
Sólo recuerdos pálidos de su amor me han dejado.
Como el labrador al ver su trabajo perdido
Vuelve al cielo los ojos esperando la lluvia,
También quiero esperar en esta hora confusa
Unas lágrimas divinas que aviven mi cosecha.

Pero hondamente fijo queda el desaliento,
Como huésped oscuro de mis sueños.
¿Puedo esperar acaso? Todo se ha dado al hombre
Tal distracción efímera de la existencia;
A nada puede unir este ansia suya que reclama
Una pausa de amor entre la fuga de las cosas.
Vano sería dolerse del trabajo, la casa, los amigos perdidos
En aquel gran negocio demoníaco de la guerra.

Estoy en la ciudad alzada para su orgullo por el rico,
Adonde la miseria oculta canta por las esquinas
O expone dibujos que me arrasan de lágrimas los ojos.
Y mordiendo mis puños con tristeza impotente
Aún cuento mentalmente mis monedas escasas,
Porque un trozo de pan aquí y unos vestidos
Suponen un esfuerzo mayor para lograrlos
Que el de los viejos héroes cuando vencían
Monstruos, rompiendo encantos con su lanza.

La revolución renace siempre, como un fénix
Llameante en el pecho de los desdichados.
Esto lo sabe el charlatán bajo los árboles
De las plazas y su baba argentina, su cascabel sonoro,

God's Visit

Now it turns out that half my life has passed.
My body is still standing and voices still whirl
And echo with withered magic in my ears,
But the slender days are long gone and far away;
All I have left are memories of their love.
Just as the farmer who's lost his work
Looks up hoping for a sign of rain,
I too want to hope in this hard time
That some heavenly tears will revive my crops.

But the drought feels settled in
Like some dark guest of my dreams.
Can I even hope? Man has been given everything
Like the passing distraction of existence;
This craving to pause for love amid everything's passing
Connects with nothing.
It would be vain to mourn lost work, lost home, friends lost
In the great demonic enterprise of war.

I'm in a city built for the pride of the rich,
Where hidden misery sings on street corners
Or displays sketches that bring tears to my eyes.
And biting my fists with impotent sadness
I still count mentally the change in my pocket
Because here a piece of bread and the clothes on your back
Are evidence of the strength required to attain them
Like that of the ancient heroes slaying monsters,
Breaking the spells of evil with their lances.

Revolution always rises again, like a phoenix
Still burning in the breasts of the losers.
The charlatan under the trees in the plaza
Knows this, and his silvery spittle, his ringing bell

Silbando entre las hojas, encanta al pueblo
Robusto y engañado con maligna elocuencia,
Y canciones de sangre acunan su miseria.

Por mi dolor comprendo que otros inmensos sufren
Hombres callados a quienes falta el ocio
Para arrojar al cielo su tormento. Mas no puedo
Copiar su enérgico silencio, que me alivia
Este consuelo de la voz, sin tierra y sin amigo,
En la profunda soledad de quien no tiene
Ya nada entre sus brazos, sino el aire en torno,
Lo mismo que un navío al alejarse sobre el mar.

¿Adónde han ido las viejas compañeras del hombre?
Mis zurcidoras de proyectos, mis tejedoras de esperanzas
Han muerto. Sus agujas y madejas reposan
Con polvo en un rincón, sin la melodía del trabajo.
Como una sombra aislada al filo de los días,
Voy repitiendo gestos y palabras mientras lejos escucho
El inmenso bostezo de los siglos pasados.

El tiempo, ese blanco desierto ilimitado,
Ese nada creadora, amenaza a los hombres
Y con luz inmortal se abre ante los deseos juveniles.
Unos quieren asir locamente su mágico reflejo,
Mas otros le conjuran con un hijo
Ofrecido en los brazos como víctima,
Porque de nueva vida se mantiene su vida
Como el agua del agua llorada por los hombres.

Pero a ti, Dios, ¿con qué te aplacaremos?
Mi sed eras tú, tú fuiste mi amor perdido,
Mi casa rota, mi vida trabajada, y la casa y la vida
De tantos hombres como yo a la deriva
En el naufragio de un país. Levantados de naipes,
Uno tras otro iban cayendo mis pobres paraísos.

Whistling through the leaves enchants the people
Tricked by a malignant eloquence
Rocking their misery to sleep with songs of blood.

For all my pain I know that others suffer
Quietly, lacking the leisure
To vent their torment. But I can't imitate
Their energetic silence, since a voice is all I have
To console and soothe me, with neither land nor friend,
In the deep solitude of someone with nothing
To embrace but the surrounding air,
Like a ship heading far out to sea.

Where have a man's old comrades gone?
My weavers of plans, my knitters of hopes
Are dead. Their needles and bolts of yarn
Lie in some dusty corner, missing the hum of work.
Like a shadow cast outside the march of time
I go on repeating myself while far away I can hear
The immense yawn of centuries gone by.

Time, that blank desert spreading in every direction,
That nothingness of creation, threatens men
But opens before the desiring young filled with immortal light.
Some try madly to seize its magical glimmerings,
But others conjure it with a child
Offered up like a victim in their arms,
Because that new life helps keep them alive
Like water distilled from human tears.

But how will we ever appease you, God?
You were my thirst, you were my lost love,
My ruined house, my belabored life, and the houses and lives
Of so many like me set adrift
By a country shipwrecked. Like houses of cards
One after another my poor paradises collapsed.

¿Movió tu mano el aire que fuera derribándolos
Y tras ellos, en el profundo abatimiento, en el hondo vacío,
Se alza al fin ante mí la nube que oculta tu presencia?

No golpees airado mi cuerpo con tu rayo;
Si el amor no eres tú, ¿quién lo será en tu mundo?
Compadécete al fin, escucha este murmullo
Que ascendiendo llega como una ola
Al pie de tu divina indiferencia.
Mira las tristes piedras que llevamos
Ya sobre nuestros hombros para enterrar tus dones:
La hermosura, la verdad, la justicia, cuyo afán imposible
Tú sólo eres capaz de infundir en nosotros.
Si ellas murieran hoy, de la memoria tú te borrarías
Como un sueño remoto de los hombres que fueron.

Was it your hand fanning the air that knocked them down
And behind them, in the great overturning, in the void,
That stirs up the cloud that hides your presence from me?

Don't get mad and strike me down with lightning;
If love is not you, who else in your world could it be?
Have pity at last, listen to this whisper
Rising to break like a wave
At the feet of your divine indifference.
Look at the pitiful stones we carry
On our backs for burying your gifts:
Beauty, truth, justice, the impossible longings
That you alone can infuse us with.
If they should perish, so would you
Like a distant dream of long since vanished men.

ATARDECER EN LA CATEDRAL

Por las calles desiertas, nadie. El viento
Y la luz sobre las tapias
Que enciende los aleros al sol último.
Tras una puerta se queja el agua oculta.
Ven a la catedral, alma de soledad temblando.

Cuando el labrador deja en esta hora
Abierta ya la tierra con los surcos,
Nace de la obra hecha gozo y calma.
Cerca de Dios se halla el pensamiento.

Algunos chopos secos, llama ardida
Levantan por el campo, como el humo
Alegre en los tejados de las casas.
Vuelve un rebaño junto al arroyo oscuro
Donde duerme la tarde entre la hierba.
El frío está naciendo y es el cielo más hondo.

Como un sueño de piedra, de música callada,
Desde la flecha erguida de la torre
Hasta la lonja de anchas losas grises,
La catedral extática aparece,
Toda reposo: vidrio, madera, bronce,
Fervor puro a la sombra de los siglos.

Una vigilia dicen esos ángeles
Y su espada desnuda sobre el pórtico,
Florido con sonrisas por los santos viejos,
Como huerto de otoño que brotara
Musgos entre las rosas esculpidas.

Aquí encuentran la paz los hombres vivos,
Paz de los odios, paz de los amores,

Nightfall in the Cathedral

Nobody on the street. A breeze,
And light reflected off the walls
Igniting the edges of the eaves at sunset.
Behind a gate a hidden fountain murmurs.
Come to the cathedral, solitary soul.

When at this hour the field hand leaves
The land turned over in furrows,
Pleasure and calm are born of the finished work.
Now thoughts turn toward God.

A few dry poplars like flames
Rise from the landscape, like the happy
Smoke pouring from chimneys.
A flock of sheep makes its way home along the shaded creek
Where afternoon is still sleeping in the grass.
It starts to get cold and the sky grows deeper.

Like a dream built of solid rock, of silent music,
From the floor's gray slabs of stone
To the proud arrow of the tower,
The cathedral appears ecstatic,
Fully at ease: stained glass, dark wood, bronze,
Pure passion in the shadow of the centuries.

Above the portico with its naked sword
Ornate with smiles of the old saints
Those angels are watching,
Like a garden in autumn sprouting
A little moss under the sculpted roses.

Here's where living men can find some peace,
Peace from their hatreds, peace from their loves,

Olvido dulce y largo, donde el cuerpo
Fatigado se baña en las tinieblas.

Entra en la catedral, ve por las naves altas
De esbelta bóveda, gratas a los pasos
Errantes sobre el mármol, entre columnas,
Hacia el altar, ascua serena,
Gloria propicia al alma solitaria.

Como el niño descansa, porque cree
En la fuerza prudente de su padre;
Con el vivir callado de las cosas
Sobre el haz inmutable de la tierra,
Transcurren estas horas en el templo.

No hay lucha ni temor, no hay pena ni deseo.
Todo queda aceptado hasta la muerte
Y olvidado tras de la muerte, contemplando,
Libres del cuerpo, y adorando,
Necesidad del alma exenta de deleite.

Apagándose van aquellos vidrios
Del alto ventanal, y apenas si con oro
Triste se irisan débilmente. Muere el día,
Pero la paz perdura postrada entre la sombra.

El suelo besan quedos unos pasos
Lejanos. Alguna forma, a solas,
Reza caída ante una vasta reja
Donde palpita el ala de una llama amarilla.

Llanto escondido moja el alma,
Sintiendo la presencia de un poder misterioso
Que el consuelo creara para el hombre,
Sombra divina hablando en el silencio.

A slow, sweet forgetting where the tired body
Is bathed in soothing shadows.

Come into the cathedral, see in the tall naves
Of the slender vault, your footsteps wandering
Pleasantly over marble, between columns,
Toward the altar, a serene glow,
A glory made for the soul in solitude.

The way a child sleeps, believing
In the protective strength of his father;
These hours inside the temple go by
With everything outside quietly alive
On the unchanging fact of the land.

No struggle, no fear, no grief, no desire.
Everyone is welcome, even death,
And forgotten after death, contemplative,
Free of the body, and worshiping,
Necessity of a soul exempt from sin.

In the stained glass of the high window
The colors are darkening, just barely a glimmer
Of sad gold faintly gleaming. Daylight dies,
But the peace settling in the dark endures.

Distant footsteps kiss the floor
In whispers. A shape, alone,
Prays on its knees before the heavy bar
Where the wing of a yellow flame is flickering.

A hidden sob drenches the soul,
Feeling the presence of a mysterious power
That might offer consolation,
The shadow of God speaking in the silence.

Aromas, brotes vivos surgen,
Afirmando la vida, tal savia de la tierra
Que irrumpe en milagrosas formas verdes,
Secreto entre los muros de este templo,
El soplo animador de nuestro mundo
Pasa y orea la noche de los hombres.

Smells of budding flowers emerge,
Affirming life, like sap from the earth
Erupting in miraculous green forms,
And secretly between this temple's walls
The animating breath of our world
Blows gently over the human night.

CORDURA

Suena la lluvia oscura.
El campo amortecido
Inclina hacia el invierno
Cimas densas de árboles.

Los cristales son bruma
Donde un iris mojado
Refleja ramas grises,
Humo de hogares, nubes.

A veces, por los claros
Del cielo, la amarilla
Luz de un edén perdido
Aún baja a las praderas.

Un hondo sentimiento
De alegrías pasadas,
Hechas olvido bajo
Tierra, llena la tarde.

Turbando el aire quieto
Con una queja ronca,
Como sombras, los cuervos
Agudos, giran, pasan.

Voces tranquilas hay
De hombres, hacia lo lejos,
Que el suelo están labrando
Como hicieron los padres.

Understanding

Dark rain is rumbling.
On the pounded countryside
Hills dense with trees
Lean toward winter.

Windows are mist
Where a wet iris
Reflects gray branches,
Wood smoke, clouds.

Sometimes, when the sky
Clears, the yellow
Light of a lost Eden
Still falls on the fields.

A deep feeling
Of past happiness,
Forgotten, under
Ground, suffuses the afternoon.

Disturbing the calm air
With raucous squawks,
Like shadows, the sharp
Crows circle and glide away.

There are people's voices,
Peaceful, a little ways off,
They're working the land
The way their fathers did.

Sus manos, si se extienden,
Hallan manos amigas.
Su fe es la misma. Juntos
Viven la misma espera.

Allá, sobre la lluvia,
Donde anidan estrellas,
Dios por su cielo mira
Dulces rincones grises.

Todo ha sido creado,
Como yo, de la sombra:
Esta tierra a mí ajena,
Estos cuerpos ajenos.

Un sueño, que conmigo
Él puso para siempre,
Me aísla. Así está el chopo
Entre encinas robustas.

Duro es hallarse solo
En medio de los cuerpos.
Pero esa forma tiene
Su amor: la cruz sin nadie.

Por ese amor espero,
Despierto en su regazo,
Hallar un alba pura
Comunión con los hombres.

Mas la luz deja el campo.
Es tarde y nace el frío.
Cerrada está la puerta,
Alumbrando la lámpara.

Their hands, when they reach out,
Find the hands of friends.
They share the same faith,
Live the same hopes, together.

Up there, above the rain,
Where the stars nest,
God in his heaven looks down
On nice gray havens.

Everything's been created,
Like me, from darkness:
This earth estranged from me,
These alien bodies.

A dream that he
Implanted in me forever
Set me apart, like a poplar
Among stout oaks.

It's hard to be alone
Amid so many bodies.
But that's the form
Love takes: a lonely cross.

That's the love I want,
To wake in its lap
And some pure daybreak find
Communion with others.

But light is leaving the land.
It's late and it's getting cold.
The door is shut,
The lamp lit.

Por las sendas sombrías
Se duele el viento ahora
Como alma aislada en lucha.
La noche será breve.

Down dark paths
The wind is in pain now
Like a soul set apart in struggle.
Night won't last long.

TRISTEZA DEL RECUERDO

Por las esquinas vagas de los sueños,
Alta la madrugada, fue conmigo
Tu imagen bien amada, como un día
En tiempos idos, cuando Dios lo quiso.

Agua ha pasado por el río abajo,
Hojas verdes perdidas llevó el viento
Desde que nuestras sombras vieron quedas
Su afán borrarse con el sol traspuesto.

Hermosa era aquella llama, breve
Como todo lo hermoso: luz y ocaso.
Vino la noche honda, y sus cenizas
Guardaron el desvelo de los astros.

Tal jugador febril ante una carta,
Un alma solitaria fue la apuesta
Arriesgada y perdida en nuestro encuentro;
El cuerpo entre los hombres quedó en pena.

¿Quién dice que se olvida? No hay olvido.
Mira a través de esta pared de hielo
Ir esa sombra hacia la lejanía
Sin el nimbo radiante del deseo.

Todo tiene su precio. Yo he pagado
El mío por aquella antigua gracia;
Y así despierto, hallando tras mi sueño
Un lecho solo, afuera yerta el alba.

Sorrow of Memory

On the deserted corner of a dream,
Sun coming up, your image I loved
Was with me, like one day
Long ago, when God wanted it that way.

Water since then is gone downriver,
Lost green leaves were blown by the wind
From which our shadows quietly watched
Their passion erased by the passing sun.

That flame was beautiful, and brief
Like everything beautiful: light and sunset.
Deep night fell, and its ashes
Watched the unveiling of the stars.

Like the feverish player of a single card,
A solitary soul was the bet placed,
Risked and lost in our encounter;
My body was left grieving among men.

Who says it's forgotten? There's no forgetting.
See on the far side of this wall of ice
That shadow fading away into the distance
Without the glowing aura of desire.

Everything has its cost. And I have paid
The price for that long gone moment of grace;
And that's how I've awakened from my dream
In an empty bed; outside, a brittle day breaks.

CANCIÓN DE INVIERNO

Tan hermoso como el fuego
Late en el ocaso quieto,
        Ardiente, dorado.

Tan hermoso como el sueño
Respira dentro del pecho,
        Solo, recatado.

Tan hermoso como el silencio
Vibra en torno de los besos,
        Alado, sagrado.

Winter Song

As beautiful as fire
Pulsing in the still sunset,
        Ardent, golden.

As beautiful as sleep
Breathing inside a chest,
        Alone, hidden.

As beautiful as silence
Vibrating in kisses,
        Winged, sacred.

LÁZARO

Era de madrugada.
Después de retirada la piedra con trabajo,
Porque no la materia sino el tiempo
Pesaba sobre ella,
Oyeron una voz tranquila
Llamándome, como un amigo llama
Cuando atrás queda alguno
Fatigado de la jornada y cae la sombra.
Hubo un silencio largo.
Así lo cuentan ellos que lo vieron.

Yo no recuerdo sino el frío
Extraño que brotaba
Desde la tierra honda, con angustia
De entresueño, y lento iba
A despertar el pecho,
Donde insistió con unos golpes leves,
Ávido de tornarse sangre tibia.
En mi cuerpo dolía
Un dolor vivo o un dolor soñado.

Era otra vez la vida.
Cuando abrí los ojos
Fue el alba pálida quien dijo
La verdad. Porque aquellos
Rostros ávidos, sobre mí estaban mudos,
Mordiendo un sueño vago inferior al milagro,
Como rebaño hosco
Que no a la voz sino a la piedra tiende,
Y el sudor de sus frentes
Oí caer pesado entre la hierba.

Lazarus

It was just before dawn.
After they managed to roll the stone away,
Because time not matter
Was weighing it down,
They heard a calm voice
Calling my name, as a friend calls out
When someone is trailing behind
Worn out by the day and the shadows are falling.
There was a long silence.
That's the way the witnesses described it.

All I can remember is the strange
Cold that seemed to spring
From deep in the ground, with the anguish
Of a nightmare, and slowly
My heart started waking,
Followed by a few weak beats
Trying to get the cool blood moving again.
My body ached
With lived pain, or pain I'd dreamed.

It was life all over again.
When I opened my eyes
It was the pale dawn that told me
The truth. Because those
Eager faces gaping at me were dumb,
Trying to get their teeth into a dream less than a miracle
Like a sullen flock
Attending not to the voice but to the stone,
And I could hear the sweat from their faces
Dripping into the grass.

Alguien dijo palabras
De nuevo nacimiento.
Mas no hubo allí sangre materna
Ni vientre fecundado
Que crea con dolor nueva vida doliente.
Sólo anchas vendas, lienzos amarillos
Con olor denso, desnudaban
La carne gris y fláccida como fruto pasado;
No el terso cuerpo oscuro, rosa de los deseos,
Sino el cuerpo de un hijo de la muerte.

El cielo rojo abría hacia lo lejos
Tras de olivos y alcores;
El aire estaba en calma.
Mas temblaban los cuerpos,
Como las ramas cuando el viento sopla,
Brotando de la noche con los brazos tendidos
Para ofrecerme su propio afán estéril.
La luz me remordía
Y hundí la frente sobre el polvo
Al sentir la pereza de la muerte.

Quise cerrar los ojos,
Buscar la vasta sombra,
La tiniebla primaria
Que su venero esconde bajo el mundo
Lavando de vergüenzas la memoria.
Cuando un alma doliente en mis entrañas
Gritó, por las oscuras galerías
Del cuerpo, agria, desencajada,
Hasta chocar contra el muro de los huesos
Y levantar mareas febriles por la sangre.

Aquel que con su mano sostenía
La lámpara testigo del milagro,
Mató brusco la llama,

Someone said something
About being born again.
But there was no mother's blood,
No fertile womb
Painfully bringing some new pain into life.
Just long bandages, yellowing sheets
With a strong smell, laying bare
The sagging gray flesh like some rotten fruit;
Not the firm dark body, flower of desire,
But the body of a child of death itself.

In the distance the sky was reddening
Beyond the hills of olive groves;
The air was calm.
But the bodies were trembling
Like branches in the wind
Coming out of the night with arms extended
Offering me their own sterile excitement.
The light made me remorseful
And feeling the torpor of death
I bent my head to the dust.

I tried to shut my eyes
In search of the vast darkness,
The primal lightlessness
That hides its origin in the underworld
Cleansing memory of its shame,
When a pained soul deep inside me
Let out a scream through the dark galleries
Of my body, jagged and uncontrollable,
Banging against my bones' walls
And setting off waves of fever through my blood.

The man holding the lamp
Witnessing the miracle
Quickly snuffed out the flame,

Porque ya el día estaba con nosotros.
Una rápida sombra sobrevino.
Entonces, hondos bajo una frente, vi unos ojos
Llenos de compasión, y hallé temblando un alma
Donde mi alma se copiaba inmensa,
Por el amor dueña del mundo.

Vi unos pies que marcaban la linde de la vida,
El borde de una túnica incolora
Plegada, resbalando
Hasta rozar la fosa, como un ala
Cuando a subir tras de la luz incita.
Sentí de nuevo el sueño, la locura
Y el error de estar vivo,
Siendo carne doliente día a día.
Pero él me había llamado
Y en mí no estaba ya sino seguirle.

Por eso, puesto en pie, anduve silencioso,
Aunque todo para mí fuera extraño y vano,
Mientras pensaba: así debieron ellos,
Muerto yo, caminar llevándome a la tierra.
La casa estaba lejos;
Otra vez vi sus muros blancos
Y el ciprés del huerto.
Sobre el terrado había una estrella pálida.
Dentro no hallamos lumbre
En el hogar cubierto de ceniza.

Todos le rodearon en la mesa.
Encontré el pan amargo, sin sabor las frutas,
El agua sin frescor, los cuerpos sin deseo;
La palabra hermandad sonaba falsa,
Y de la imagen del amor quedaban
Sólo recuerdos vagos bajo el viento.

Because day had broken.
A swift shadow passed over us.
Then I saw eyes full of compassion
Under a deep brow, and found a trembling soul
Mirroring my soul as if infinitely
Guarding the world with its vast love.

I saw some feet marking life's limit,
The edge of a faded tunic,
Its folds brushing
The gravestone, like a wing
Startled into flight by daylight.
Again it felt like a dream, like madness
And a mistake to be alive,
To be suffering flesh one day after another.
But he had called me
And I had no choice but to follow.

That's why I got up and started to walk, not speaking,
Even though everything felt strange and purposeless,
While I thought: that's how they should have walked
Carrying me to the grave when I was dead.
I could see the white walls
Of home again in the distance
And the cypress in the garden.
There was a faded star above the plot.
Inside we found no light
In the fireplace ashes.

Everyone was assembled around the table.
I found the bread bitter, the fruit without flavor,
The water stale, the bodies sexless;
The word brotherhood sounded false,
And all that was left of love's image
Were misty memories scattered in the wind.

Él conocía que todo estaba muerto
En mí, que yo era un muerto
Andando entre los muertos.

Sentado a su derecha me veía
Como aquel que festejan al retorno.
La mano suya descansaba cerca
Y incliné la frente sobre ella
Con asco de mi cuerpo y de mi alma.
Así pedí en silencio, como se pide
A Dios, porque su nombre,
Más vasto que los templos, los mares, las estrellas,
Cabe en el desconsuelo del hombre que está solo,
Fuerza para llevar la vida nuevamente.

Así rogué, con lágrimas,
Fuerza de soportar mi ignorancia resignado,
Trabajando, no por mi vida ni mi espíritu,
Mas por una verdad en aquellos ojos entrevista
Ahora. La hermosura es paciencia.
Sé que el lirio del campo,
Tras de su humilde oscuridad en tantas noches
Con larga espera bajo tierra,
Del tallo verde erguido a la corola alba
Irrumpe un día en gloria triunfante.

He knew that everything in me
Was dead, that I was a dead man
Walking among the dead.

He could see me seated at his right
Like someone celebrated on his return.
His hand was resting nearby
And I lay my head down on it,
Sick of my own body and of my soul.
And so I beseeched in silence, as one beseeches
God, because his name,
Though vaster than temples or seas or stars,
Fits inside a lonely man's despair
And gives him the strength to bear his life again.

And so I prayed, in tears,
For the strength to bear my ignorance with resignation,
Toiling not for my life nor for my spirit
But for a truth I could now make out in those eyes.
Beauty is patience.
I know the lily in the field,
After its humble obscurity so many nights,
After its long wait under the earth,
On a green stem rising to a dawnlike corolla,
Opens one day in victorious glory.

IMPRESIÓN DE DESTIERRO

Fue la pasada primavera,
Hace ahora casi un año,
En un salón del viejo Temple, en Londres,
Con viejos muebles. Las ventanas daban,
Tras edificios viejos, a lo lejos,
Entre la hierba el gris relámpago del río.
Todo era gris y estaba fatigado
Igual que el iris de una perla enferma.

Eran señores viejos, viejas damas,
En los sombreros plumas polvorientas;
Un susurro de voces allá por los rincones,
Junto a mesas con tulipanes amarillos,
Retratos de familia y teteras vacías.
La sombra que caía
Con un olor a gato,
Despertaba ruidos en cocinas.

Un hombre silencioso estaba
Cerca de mí. Veía
La sombra de su largo perfil algunas veces
Asomarse abstraído al borde de la taza,
Con la misma fatiga
Del muerto que volviera
Desde la tumba a una fiesta mundana.

En los labios de alguno,
Allá por los rincones
Donde los viejos juntos susurraban,
Densa como una lágrima cayendo,
Brotó de pronto una palabra: España.

Impression of Exile

It was last spring,
Nearly a year now,
In the salon of the old Temple, in London,
With its old furniture. The windows looked out,
Past old buildings, in the distance,
Between the lawns, on a gray zigzag of river.
Everything was gray and looked tired
Like the dull sheen of a sick pearl.

There were elderly gentlemen, old ladies
With dusty feathers in their hats;
A murmur of voices coming from the corners
Near tables with yellow tulips,
Family portraits and empty teapots.
The shadows falling
With a catlike smell
Were stirring up sounds in kitchens.

A very quiet man was seated
Near me. I could see
The shadow of his long profile at times
Looking up absently from the rim of his cup,
With the same weariness
Of a corpse coming back
From the grave to some mundane gathering.

From someone's lips,
Over in a corner
Where clusters of old folks were talking,
Heavy as a falling teardrop,
Came one word: Spain.

Un cansancio sin nombre
Rodaba en mi cabeza.
Encendieron las luces. Nos marchamos.

Tras largas escaleras casi a oscuras
Me hallé luego en la calle,
Y a mi lado, al volverme,
Vi otra vez a aquel hombre silencioso,
Que habló indistinto algo
Con acento extranjero,
Un acento de niño en voz envejecida.

Andando me seguía
Como si fuera solo bajo un peso invisible,
Arrastrando la losa de su tumba;
Mas luego se detuvo.
"¿España?", dijo. "Un nombre.
España ha muerto." Había
Una súbita esquina en la calleja.
Le vi borrarse entre la sombra húmeda.

An unspeakable fatigue
Circled my skull.
The lights came on. We left.

After descending long dim flights of stairs
I found myself in the street,
And next to me, when I turned,
I saw that quiet man again,
Who said something I didn't quite get
In a foreign accent,
A child's accent in a voice grown old.

He followed me, walking
As if all alone beneath an invisible weight,
Shouldering his own gravestone;
But then he stopped.
"Spain?" he said. "A name.
Spain is dead." The little street
Suddenly turned a corner.
I watched him disappear into the damp shadows.

CEMENTERIO EN LA CIUDAD

Tras de la reja abierta entre los muros,
La tierra negra sin árboles ni hierba,
Con bancos de madera donde allá a la tarde
Se sientan silenciosos unos viejos.
En torno están las casas, cerca hay tiendas,
Calles por las que juegan niños, y los trenes
Pasan al lado de las tumbas. Es un barrio pobre.

Como remiendos de las fachadas grises,
Cuelgan en las ventanas trapos húmedos de lluvia.
Borradas están ya las inscripciones
De las losas con muertos de dos siglos,
Sin amigos que les olviden, muertos
Clandestinos. Mas cuando el sol despierta,
Porque el sol brilla algunos días hacia junio,
En lo hondo algo deben sentir los huesos viejos.

Ni una hoja ni un pájaro. La piedra nada más. La tierra.
¿Es el inferno así? Hay dolor sin olvido,
Con ruido y miseria, frío largo y sin esperanza.
Aquí no existe el sueño silencioso
De la muerte, que todavía la vida
Se agita entre estas tumbas, como una prostituta
Prosigue su negocio bajo la noche inmóvil.

Cuando la sombra cae desde el cielo nublado
Y el humo de las fábricas se aquieta
En polvo gris, vienen de la taberna voces,
Y luego un tren que pasa
Agita largos ecos como bronce iracundo.
No es el juicio aún, muertos anónimos.
Sosegaos, dormid; dormid si es que podéis.
Acaso Dios también se olvida de vosotros.

Cemetery in the City

Behind the wrought iron gates between the walls,
Just black ground, no trees or even grass,
With wooden benches where a few old men
Are sitting quietly in the afternoon.
There are houses all around, stores close by,
Streets where children are playing, and the trains
Go by not far from the graves. It's a poor neighborhood.

Like patches on the gray façades,
Rain dampened rags hang in windows.
The inscriptions on the gravestones
Of two centuries of the dead are worn away,
With no friends to forget them, unknowable
Dead. But when the sun comes out,
Because the sun does shine for a few days around June,
The old bones underground should be able to feel something.

Not a leaf, not a bird. Nothing but stone. Earth.
Is this what hell is like? Pain that never ends,
Noise, misery, endless hopeless cold.
Here the silent sleep of death
Does not exist, because life is still
Shivering among the graves, the way a prostitute
Carries on with her business under the frozen night.

When darkness falls through the overcast
And the smoke from the factories settles
Into a gray dust, voices come out of the pub,
And then a passing train
Shakes out long echoes like an angry horn.
It's not yet Judgment Day, nameless dead ones.
Try to relax, sleep; sleep if you can.
It could be God has also forgotten you.

JARDÍN ANTIGUO

Ir de nuevo al jardín cerrado,
Que tras los arcos de la tapia,
Entre magnolios, limoneros,
Guarda el encanto de las aguas.

Oír de nuevo en el silencio,
Vivo de trinos y de hojas,
El susurro tibio del aire
Donde las almas viejas flotan.

Ver otra vez el cielo hondo
A lo lejos, la torre esbelta
Tal flor de luz sobre las palmas:
Las cosas todas siempre bellas.

Sentir otra vez, como entonces,
La espina aguda del deseo,
Mientras la juventud pasada
Vuelve. Sueño de un dios sin tiempo.

Ancient Garden

Enter that bounded garden again,
Where through the arches of its walls
Among magnolias and lemon trees
The spell of running water waits.

Hear in that quiet place again,
Alive with birdsong and with leaves,
The gentle rustling of the air
Where old souls hover silently.

See that deep blue sky again,
The slender tower just beyond,
A flower of light above the palms:
All those always lovely things.

Feel again, the same as then,
The sharp pain of desire's thorn,
While your vanished youth returns.
Dream of a god outside time.

DESEO

Por el campo tranquilo de septiembre,
Del álamo amarillo alguna hoja,
Como una estrella rota,
Girando al suelo viene.

Si así el alma inconsciente,
Señor de las estrellas y las hojas,
Fuese, encendida sombra,
De la vida a la muerte.

Desire

Like a star broken out of the sky,
Some yellow leaf of the poplar
Swirls down and lands on the ground
In the calm countryside of September.

If only the unknowing soul,
Lord of the stars and the leaves,
Were like that, the spark of a shadow
Falling from life into death.

AMOR OCULTO

Como el tumulto gris del mar levanta
Un alto arco de espuma, maravilla
Multiforme del agua, y ya en la orilla
Roto, otra nueva espuma se adelanta;

Como el campo despierta en primavera
Eternamente, fiel bajo el sombrío
Celaje de las nubes, y al sol frío
Con asfodelos cubre la pradera;

Como el genio en distintos cuerpos nace,
Formas que han de nutrir la antigua gloria
De su fuego, mientras la humana escoria
Sueña ardiendo en la llama y se deshace,

Así siempre, como agua, flor o llama,
Vuelves entre la sombra, fuerza oculta
Del otro amor. El mundo bajo insulta.
Pero la vida es tuya: surge y ama.

Love from the Shadows

As the ocean's gray violence throws into the air
A flying arc of spray, a shapeshifting
Watery marvel, and broken on the shore,
Another wave of foam advances;

As in the countryside spring awakens
Eternally, faithful beneath the dark
Brow of the clouds, and under the cold sun
Covers the fields with asphodels;

As genius is born in different bodies,
Forms made to feed the ancient glory
Of its fire, while human ashes
Dream of burning in its flame and fall apart,

So always, like water or flowers or flame,
You return among shadows, shadowy force
Of a different love. The lowly world hurls insults.
But life belongs to you: rise up and love.

GAVIOTAS EN LOS PARQUES

Dueña de los talleres, las fábricas, los bares,
Toda piedras oscuras bajo un cielo sombrío,
Silenciosa a la noche, los domingos devota,
Es la ciudad levítica que niega sus pecados.

El verde turbio de la hierba y los árboles
Interrumpe con parques los edificios uniformes,
Y en la naturaleza sin encanto, entre la lluvia,
Mira de pronto, penacho de locura, las gaviotas.

¿Por qué, teniendo alas, son huéspedes del humo,
El sucio arroyo, los puentes de madera de estos parques?
Un viento de infortunio o una mano inconsciente,
De los puertos nativos, tierra adentro las trajo.

Lejos quedó su nido de los mares, mecido por tormentas
De invierno, en calma luminosa los veranos.
Ahora su queja va, como el grito de almas en destierro.
Quien con alas las hizo, el espacio les niega.

Seagulls in the Parks

Mistress of shops, of factories and pubs,
Nothing but dark stones under the overcast,
Silent at night, pious on Sundays,
The churchly city denies its sins.

Green disturbances of grass and trees,
Parks disrupt these blocks of identical buildings,
And under the rain, in disenchanted nature,
Look! A sudden spray of madness: wheeling gulls.

Why, with their wings, would they be drawn to the smog,
The filthy streams, the wooden bridges of these parks?
An ill wind or some ignorant hand
Has swept them inland from their native ports.

Their nests on the ocean are far away, tossed
By winter storms, calmed by summer sun.
Now their call goes out, like the cry of souls in exile.
Whoever gave them wings, space has disowned them.

UN ESPAÑOL HABLA DE SU TIERRA

Las playas, parameras
Al rubio sol durmiendo,
Los oteros, las vegas
En paz, a solas, lejos;

Los castillos, ermitas,
Cortijos y conventos,
La vida con la historia,
Tan dulces al recuerdo,

Ellos, los vencedores
Caínes sempiternos,
De todo me arrancaron.
Me dejan el destierro.

Una mano divina
Tu tierra alzó en mi cuerpo
Y allí la voz dispuso
Que hablase tu silencio.

Contigo solo estaba,
En ti sola creyendo;
Pensar tu nombre ahora
Envenena mis sueños.

Amargos son los días
De la vida, viviendo
Sólo una larga espera
A fuerza de recuerdos.

A Spaniard Speaks of His Land

The beaches flat and empty
Asleep in the blond sunlight,
The hills, the serene dunes
All alone in the distance;

The castles, monasteries,
Farmhouses and convents,
Life with its history,
So sweet in memory,

And they, the conquering
Everlasting Cains,
Uprooted me from it all
And left me in exile.

The hand of some god raised
Your earth inside my body
And ordered my voice
To speak your silences.

I was alone with you,
Believing only in you;
To think of your name now
Poisons my dreams.

The days of life are bitter
When living is merely waiting
And hoping for so long
On the strength of memories.

Un día, tú ya libre
De la mentira de ellos,
Me buscarás. Entonces
¿Qué ha de decir un muerto?

One day when you're free
Of all their lies, you'll come
Looking for me. But then
What can a dead man say?

PÁJARO MUERTO

Sobre la tierra gris de la colina,
Bajo las hojas nuevas del espino,
Al pie de la cancela donde pasan
Jóvenes estudiantes en toga roja,

Rota estaba tu ala blanca y negra,
Inmóvil en la muerte. Parecías
Una rosa cortada, o una estrella
Desterrada del trono de la noche.

Aquella forma inerte fue un día al vuelo
Extasiado en la luz, el canto ardiente
De amanecer, la paz nocturna
Del nido allá en la cima.

Inútil ya todo parece, tal parece
La pena del amor cuando se ha ido,
El sufrir por lo bello que envejece,
El afán de la luz que anegan sombras.

Si como el mar, que de su muerte nace,
Fueras tú. Una forma espectral de ti vislumbro
Que llora entre los aires los amores
Breves y hermosos de tus días idos.

Ahora, silencio. Duerme. Olvida todo.
Nutre de ti la muerte que en ti anida.
Esa quietud del ala, como un sol poniente,
Acaso es de la vida una forma más alta.

Dead Bird

On the gray ground of the hillside,
Under the new leaves of the hawthorn,
At the foot of the grillwork
Where red robed students pass,

Your black and white wing was broken,
Motionless in death. You looked like
A cut rose, or a star
In exile from night's throne.

That lifeless form was once ecstatic
Flight in sunlight, daybreak's
Ardent song, nocturnal peace
Of the nest in the treetop.

Now it all seems pointless, the way
Love's sorrows seem once love is gone,
The suffering for beauty that grows old,
Passion for light negated by the dark.

If only you could be like the ocean,
Born of its own death. I catch a glimpse
Of your ghostly form weeping for the brief
And beautiful loves of your lost years.

Quiet now. Sleep. Forget everything.
Let death make its nest and be nourished in you.
That stilled wing, like a setting sun,
May well be a higher form of life.

EL RUISEÑOR SOBRE LA PIEDRA

Lirio sereno en piedra erguido
Junto al huerto monástico pareces.
Ruiseñor claro entre los pinos
Que un canto silencioso levantara.
O fruto de granada, recio afuera,
Mas propicio y jugoso en lo escondido.
Así, Escorial, te mira mi recuerdo.
Si hacia los cielos anchos te alzas duro,
Sobre el agua serena del estanque
Hecho gracias sonríes. Y las nubes
Coronan tus designios inmortales.

Recuerdo bien el sur donde el olivo crece
Junto al mar claro y el cortijo blanco,
Mas hoy va mi recuerdo más arriba, a la sierra
Gris bajo el cielo azul, cubierta de pinares,
Y allí encuentro regazo, alma con alma.
Mucho enseña el destierro de nuestra propia tierra.
¿Qué saben de ella quienes la gobiernan?
¿Quiénes obtienen de ella
Fácil vivir con un social renombre?
De ella también somos los hijos
Oscuros. Como el mar, no mira
Qué aguas son las que van perdidas a sus aguas,
Y el cuerpo, que es de tierra, clama por su tierra.

Porque me he perdido
En el tiempo lo mismo que en la vida,
Sin cosa propia, fe ni gloria,
Entre gentes ajenas
Y sobre ajeno suelo
Cuyo polvo no es el de mi cuerpo;

Nightingale on a Rock

You look serene as a stone lily
Standing beside the monastery gardens.
A bright nightingale among the pines
Lifting a silent song.
Or a pomegranate, hard on the outside,
Succulent within.
That's how my memory sees you, Escorial.
If you thrust yourself firmly into the open sky,
On the smooth water of the pond
Your smile is kind. And clouds
Crown your undying design.

I remember well the south with its olive groves
Next to the bright ocean and the white farmhouses,
But today my memory turns north to the gray
Mountains beneath a blue sky, covered with pines,
And that's where it finds comfort, soul to soul.
Exile teaches us a lot about our own land.
What do the ones who are ruling it know?
The ones who make of it
A good living and a reputation?
But we darker children also belong
To her. Like the ocean, she doesn't notice
What waters are lost in her waters,
And the body, made of earth, longs for its land.

Because I've gotten lost
In time the same as in life,
With nothing to my name, no faith, no fame,
Living among strangers
On foreign soil
Whose dust is different from my body's dust;

No con el pensamiento vuelto a lo pasado,
Ni con la fiebre ilusa del futuro,
Sino con el sosiego casi triste
De quien mira a lo lejos, de camino,
Las tapias que de niño le guardaran
Dorarse al sol caído de la tarde,
A ti, Escorial, me vuelvo.

Hay quienes aman los cuerpos
Y aquellos que las almas aman.
Hay también los enamorados de las sombras
Como poder y gloria. O quienes aman
Sólo a sí mismos. Yo también he amado
En otro tiempo alguna de esas cosas,
Mas después me sentí a solas con mi tierra,
Y la amé, porque algo debe amarse
Mientras dura la vida. Pero en la vida todo
Huye cuando el amor quiere fijarlo.
Así también mi tierra la he perdido,
Y si hoy hablo de ti es buscando recuerdos
En el trágico ocio del poeta.

Tus muros no los veo
Con estos ojos míos,
Ni mis manos los tocan.
Están aquí, dentro de mí, tan claros,
Que con su luz borran la sombra
Nórdica donde estoy, y me devuelven
A la sierra granítica en que sueñas
Inmóvil, por la verde foscura de los montes
Brillando al sol como un acero limpio,
Desnudo y puro como carne efímera,
Pero tu entraña es dura, hermana de los dioses.

It isn't with my thoughts turned toward the past
Nor with an illusory fever for the future,
But with a kind of melancholy calm
Of someone who can see in the distance, from the road,
The roofs that protected him as a child
Turning golden in the sun of late afternoon,
That I return to you, Escorial.

There are those who love bodies
And those who love souls.
There are also the lovers of shadows
Like power and fame. Or those who love
Only themselves. There was a time
When I too loved some of these things,
But later I felt alone with my land,
And I loved her, because you should love something
While life lasts. But in life everything
Escapes love's efforts to hold it.
That's how I too have lost my land.
And if I speak of you it is in search of memories
Here in a poet's tragic idleness.

I can't see your walls
With these eyes of mine,
And my hands can't touch them.
But they're here, inside me, so bright
Their light can wipe out the northern
Darkness where I am, and they return me
To the granite mountain where you dream,
Still, on the dark green of the rock
Shining in the sun like a clean blade,
Naked and pure as ephemeral flesh,
But your core is solid, sister of the gods.

Eres alegre, con gozo mesurado
Hecho de impulso y de recogimiento,
Que no comprende el hombre si no ha sido
Hermano de tus nubes y tus piedras.
Vivo estás como el aire
Abierto de montaña,
Como el verdor desnudo
De solitarias cimas,
Como los hombres vivos
Que te hicieron un día,
Alzando en ti la imagen
De la alegría humana,
Dura porque no pase,
Muda porque es un sueño.

Agua esculpida eres,
Música helada en piedra.
La roca te levanta
Como un ave en los aires;
Piedra, columna, ala
Erguida al sol, cantando
Las palabras de un himno,
El himno de los hombres
Que no supieron cosas útiles
Y despreciaron cosas prácticas.
¿Qué es lo útil, lo práctico,
Sino la vieja añagaza diabólica
De esclavizar al hombre
Al infierno en el mundo?

Tú, hermosa imagen nuestra,
Eres inútil como el lirio.
Pero ¿cuáles ojos humanos
Sabrían prescindir de una flor viva?
Junto a una sola hoja de hierba,

You're happy, with measured pleasure
Composed of impulse and fulfillment,
Which no man can understand who hasn't been
Brother to your clouds, your stones.
You are alive like the open
Mountain air,
Like the naked green
Of solitary peaks,
Like the living men
Who built you one day,
Erecting you in the image
Of human joy,
Enduring, not passing,
Soundless because it's a dream.

You are sculpted water,
Music frozen in stone.
The rock raises you up
Like a bird into the sky;
Stone, column, wing
Raised toward the sun, singing
The words of a hymn,
The hymn of men
Who didn't know how to do anything useful
And had no use for practical things.
What is useful, or practical,
But the old diabolical trap
Of man's enslavement
To hell on earth?

You, our beautiful image,
Are as useless as a lily.
But what human eyes
Could live without fresh flowers?
Next to a single blade of grass,

¿Qué vale el horrible mundo práctico
Y útil, pesadilla del norte,
Vómito de la niebla y el fastidio?
Lo hermoso es lo que pasa
Negándose a servir. Lo hermoso, lo que amamos,
Tú sabes que es un sueño y que por eso
Es más hermoso aún para nosotros.

Tú conoces las horas
Largas del ocio dulce,
Pasadas en vivir de cara al cielo
Cantando el mundo bello, obra divina,
Con voz que nadie oye
Ni busca aplauso humano,
Como el ruiseñor canta
En la noche de estío,
Porque su sino quiere
Que cante, porque su amor le impulsa.
Y en la gloria nocturna
Divinamente solo
Sube su canto puro a las estrellas.

Así te canto ahora, porque eres
Alegre, con trágica alegría
Titánica de piedras que enlaza la armonía,
Al coro de montañas sujetándola.
Porque eres la vida misma
Nuestra, mas no perecedera,
Sino eterna, con sus tercos anhelos
Conseguidos por siempre y nuevos siempre
Bajo una luz sin sombras.
Y si tu imagen tiembla en las aguas tendidas,
Es tan sólo una imagen;

What is the horrible useful practical
World of the north worth,
Vomiting its fog and its disgust?
The beautiful is what drifts past
Refusing to serve a purpose.
What's beautiful, what we love, you know it's a dream
And that's why to us it's even more beautiful.

You understand the long
Sweet hours of doing nothing,
Spent looking up at the sky
Singing the lovely world, work of the gods,
In a voice nobody hears
That isn't looking for applause,
The way a nightingale sings
On a summer night
Because it's his fate
To sing, because his love inspires him.
And under the glory of night
Divinely alone
His pure song rises toward the stars.

That's why I'm singing now, because you are
Joyful, with the tragic
Titanic joy of stones bound in harmony,
With the chorus of mountains holding it in place.
Because you are to us our very
Life, not perishing
But eternal, with your stubborn desires
Forever fulfilled and always new
Beneath a light without shadows.
And if your image trembles in the water's surface,
It's only an image;

Y si el tiempo nos lleva, ahogando tanto afán insatisfecho,
Es sólo como un sueño;
Que ha de vivir tu voluntad de piedra,
Ha de vivir, y nosotros contigo.

And if time sweeps us downstream drowning so much thwarted
passion,
It's only as a dream;
Your will of stone is bound to live,
To live, and we with you.

Translator's note: El Escorial, in the foothills of the Sierra de Guadarrama, northwest of Madrid, is the sixteenth-century monastery erected by King Philip II, one of the masterworks of Spanish architecture.

from

Como Quien Espera el Alba

Like Someone Awaiting Dawn

[1941–1944]

LAS RUINAS

Silencio y soledad nutren la hierba
Creciendo oscura y fuerte entre ruinas,
Mientras la golondrina con grito enajenado
Va por el aire vasto, y bajo el viento
Las hojas en las ramas tiemblan vagas
Como al roce de cuerpos invisibles.

Puro, de plata nebulosa, ya levanta
El agudo creciente de la luna
Vertiendo por el campo paz amiga,
Y en esta luz incierta las ruinas de mármol
Son construcciones bellas, musicales,
Que el sueño completó.

Esto es el hombre. Mira
La avenida de tumbas y cipreses, y las calles
Llevando al corazón de la gran plaza
Abierta a un horizonte de colinas:
Todo está igual, aunque una sombra sea
De lo que fue hace siglos, mas sin gente.

Levanta ese titánico acueducto
Arcos rotos y secos por el valle agreste
Adonde el mirto crece con la anémona,
En tanto el agua libre entre los juncos
Pasa con la enigmática elocuencia
De su hermosura que venció a la muerte.

En las tumbas vacías, las urnas sin cenizas,
Conmemoran aún relieves delicados
Muertos que ya no son sino la inmensa muerte anónima,
Aunque sus prendas leves sobrevivan:

The Ruins

Silence and solitude nourish the grass
Growing dark and strong among the ruins,
While the swallow with its ecstatic cry
Swoops through the vast sky, and the leaves
On the branches subtly tremble in the wind
As if being grazed by invisible bodies.

A sharp edged crescent moon is rising,
A pure and cloudy silver, pouring
Its friendly calm over the landscape,
And in this strange light the marble ruins
Are beautiful, musical structures
Built by dreams.

                    This is humanity. Look
Down that avenue of tombs and cypresses, and the streets
Flowing into the heart of the great plaza
Open to the hills on the horizon:
Everything is the same, if only a shadow
Of what it was centuries ago, and empty of people.

That gigantic aqueduct
Raises its dry broken arches out of the rugged valley
Where myrtle grows, and anemones,
Just as the water moving among the reeds
Flows past with the enigmatic eloquence
Of its beauty, which has defeated death.

On the empty tombs, the urns without ashes,
Finely carved reliefs go on commemorating
The dead now nothing more than nameless enormous death,
Though some of their prize possessions survive:

Pomos ya sin perfume, sortijas y joyeles
O el talismán irónico de un sexo poderoso,
Que el trágico desdén del tiempo perdonara.

Las piedras que los pies vivos rozaron
En centurias atrás, aún permanecen
Quietas en su lugar, y las columnas
En la plaza, testigos de las luchas políticas,
Y los altares donde sacrificaron y esperaron,
Y los muros que el placer de los cuerpos recataban.

Tan sólo ellos no están. Este silencio
Parece que aguardase la vuelta de sus vidas.
Mas los hombres, hechos de esa materia fragmentaria
Con que se nutre el tiempo, aunque sean
Aptos para crear lo que resiste al tiempo,
Ellos en cuya mente lo eterno se concibe,
Como en fruto el hueso encierran muerte.

Oh Dios. Tú que nos has hecho
Para morir, ¿por qué nos infundiste
La sed de eternidad, que hace al poeta?
¿Puedes dejar así, siglo tras siglo,
Caer como vilanos que deshace un soplo
Los hijos de la luz en la tiniebla avara?

Mas tú no existes. Eres tan sólo el nombre
Que da el hombre a su miedo y su impotencia,
Y la vida sin ti es esto que parecen
Estas mismas ruinas bellas en su abandono:
Delirio de la luz ya sereno a la noche,
Delirio acaso hermoso cuando es corto y es leve.

Todo lo que es hermoso tiene su instante, y pasa.
Importa como eterno gozar de nuestro instante.
Yo no te envidio, Dios; déjame a solas

Flasks now without perfume, rings, jewels,
Or the ironic symbol of a powerful phallus,
Which has perhaps forgiven the tragic neglect of time.

The stones where living feet once stepped
In centuries past are still here
Quietly in place, and the columns
In the plaza, witness to political struggles,
And the altars where they sacrificed and waited,
And the walls that once concealed the pleasure of bodies.

Only they are no longer here. This silence
Seems to guard against their return.
Yet humans, made of that fragmentary matter
Time feeds on, though they're
Clever enough to create what defies time,
The ones who thought up the idea of eternity,
Contain death like the stone inside the fruit.

Oh God. You who have made us
Only to die, why did you infuse us
With this thirst for eternity the poet suffers?
How can you allow, one age after another,
Children of light to drop into the dark
Like thistles blown down by a breeze?

And yet you don't exist. You're just the name
Man gives to his fear and his impotence,
And life without you is the same as this
That these beautiful ruins resemble in their desolation:
Enraptured calm of this falling night,
Rapturous beauty, so brief, so light.

Everything beautiful has its moment, and passes.
It gives us eternal pleasure in that moment.
I feel no envy for you, God; leave me alone

Con mis obras humanas que no duran:
El afán de llenar lo que es efímero
De eternidad, vale tu omnipotencia.

Esto es el hombre. Aprende pues, y cesa
De perseguir eternos dioses sordos
Que tu plegaria nutre y tu olvido aniquila.
Tu vida, lo mismo que la flor, ¿es menos bella acaso
Porque crezca y se abra en brazos de la muerte?

Sagrada y misteriosa cae la noche,
Dulce como una mano amiga que acaricia,
Y en su pecho, donde tal ahora yo, otros un día
Descansaron la frente, me reclino
A contemplar sereno el campo y las ruinas.

With my human works that don't last:
The desire to fill the ephemeral with eternity
Is equal to your omnipotence.

This is humanity. Learn that, and leave off
Pursuing those eternally deaf gods
Who feed on your pleas and who your forgetting obliterates.
Is your life, like a flower's, any less beautiful
Because it grows and opens in the arms of death?

Night is falling, mysterious and sacred,
Softly as an intimate caress,
And on its breast where others
Once lay their heads, I now lay mine
And calmly contemplate the landscape and the ruins.

JUVENTUD

¿Es más bella la hoja
Verde, que su deseo?
¿Luz estival de oro,
O nimbo de embeleso?

Mejor que la palabra,
El silencio en que duerme.
No la pasión: el sueño
Adonde está latente.

Al ser irreductible,
La nube primitiva
Prefiere; las futuras
Criaturas divinas.

Esa indecisa gracia
Tan pura de la fuente,
No el mar; y esa sonrisa
Que al amor antecede.

No el arco triunfante
De meta conseguida:
La inicial misteriosa
Y eterna de la vida.

Youth

Which is lovelier,
The leaf or its desire?
The golden light of summer
Or the glow of its enchantment?

Better than the word
Is the silence where it sleeps.
Not passion but the dream
Where it pulses, hidden.

Youth prefers the primal
Cloud to the actual
Person; the divine creatures
Promised by the future.

That pure uncertain grace
Burbling in a spring,
Not the ocean; and the smile
That precedes and promises love.

Not the victorious arch
Of the accomplished deed:
But the mysterious and
Eternal beginning of life.

OFRENDA

Para que los dioses te fueran
Propicios, más de una guirnalda,
Romero, mirto, mejorana,
Les has tejido en primavera.

Cuando el invierno venga, ¿dónde
Tu mano ha de encontrar las hojas,
Tus ojos una luz sin sombras,
Tu amor su forma en cuerpo joven?

Esa pobreza es grata al cielo:
Deja a los dioses en ofrenda,
Tal grano vivo que se siembra,
La desnudez de tu deseo.

Offering

So that the gods might be good
To you, it takes more than a garland
Of rosemary, myrtle and marjoram
You've woven for them in spring.

When winter comes, where
Will your hand find the leaves,
Your eyes a light without shadows,
Your love its form, a young body?

That poverty pleases heaven:
Make the gods an offering,
Like living seed you sow,
Of your naked desire.

TIERRA NATIVA

A Paquita G. de la Bárcena

Es la luz misma, la que abrió mis ojos
Toda ligera y tibia como un sueño,
Sosegada en colores delicados
Sobre las formas puras de las cosas.

El encanto de aquella tierra llana,
Extendida como una mano abierta,
Adonde el limonero encima de la fuente
Suspendía su fruto entre el ramaje.

El muro viejo en cuya barda abría
A la tarde su flor azul la enredadera,
Y al cual la golondrina en el verano
Tornaba siempre hacia su antiguo nido.

El susurro del agua alimentando,
Con su música insomne en el silencio,
Los sueños que la vida aún no corrompe,
El futuro que espera como página blanca.

Todo vuelve otra vez vivo a la mente,
Irreparable ya con el andar del tiempo,
Y su recuerdo ahora me traspasa
El pecho tal puñal fino y seguro.

Raíz del tronco verde, ¿quién la arranca?
Aquel amor primero, ¿quién lo vence?
Tu sueño, y tu recuerdo, ¿quién lo olvida,
Tierra nativa, más mía cuanto más lejana?

Native Land

for Paquita G. de la Bárcena

It is light itself that opened my eyes
Completely weightless, warm as a dream,
Peacefully shedding delicate colors
Over the virgin forms of everything.

A spell was cast by that flat land
Spread out for me like an open hand,
Where a lemon tree beside a fountain
Held on its branch its fragrant fruit.

The old wall whose thatched top revealed
Its web of blue flowers to the afternoon,
And where the swallows in summertime
Always returned to their old nests.

The murmur of water forever feeding,
With its sleepless music in the silence,
Dreams as yet unspoiled by living,
The future like a white page waiting.

Everything comes again to mind,
Irreparable now with passing time,
And its memory now enters my heart
Like a knife whose blade and point are sharp.

Roots of the green trunk, who could uproot them?
That first love, who could defeat it?
Your dream, your memory, who could forget it?
My native land, more mine the more distant?

GÓNGORA

El andaluz envejecido que tiene gran razón para su orgullo,
El poeta cuya palabra lúcida es como diamante,
Harto de fatigar sus esperanzas por la corte,
Harto de su pobreza noble que le obliga
A no salir de casa cuando el día, sino al atardecer, ya que
las sombras,
Más generosas que los hombres, disimulan
En la común tiniebla parda de las calles
La bayeta caduca de su coche y el tafetán delgado de su traje;
Harto de pretender favores de magnates,
Su altivez humillada por el ruego insistente,
Harto de los años tan largos malgastados
En perseguir fortuna lejos de Córdoba la llana y de su
muro excelso,
Vuelve al rincón nativo para morir tranquilo y silencioso.

Ya restituye el alma a soledad sin esperar de nadie
Si no es de su conciencia, y menos todavía
De aquel sol invernal de la grandeza
Que no atempera el frío del desdichado,
Y aprende a desearles buen viaje
A príncipes, virreyes, duques altisonantes,
Vulgo luciente no menos estúpido que el otro;
Ya se resigna a ver pasar la vida tal sueño inconsistente
Que el alba desvanece, a amar el rincón solo
Adonde conllevar paciente su pobreza,
Olvidando que tantos menos dignos que él, como la bestia ávida
Toman hasta saciarse la parte mejor de toda cosa,
Dejándole la amarga, el desecho del paria.

Pero en la poesía encontró siempre, no tan sólo hermosura,
sino ánimo,
La fuerza del vivir más libre y más soberbio,

Góngora

The old Andalusian whose pride is fully justified,
The poet whose lucid language shines like diamonds,
Sick and tired of wearing out his hopes before the court,
Sick of his noble poverty that keeps him
From venturing out in daylight, but only at dusk, since shadows,
More benevolent than men, conceal
In the common darkness of the streets
The ragged curtains of his coach and the threadbare silk of his
  clothes;
Sick of asking favors of the powerful,
His stature diminished by relentless begging,
Sick of the long years ill spent
In pursuit of fortune far from Córdoba the plain and its
  glorious wall,
He returns to his place of birth to die in peace and quiet.

Now he restores his soul in solitude expecting nothing of anyone
Not of his own conscience, and still less
From that wintery sun of greatness
That does nothing to warm the cold of the outcast,
And he learns to wish safe travels
To princes, viceroys, arrogant dukes,
Illustrious nobodies no less stupid than the rest;
By now he's resigned to watching life pass like a flimsy dream
Broken up by daybreak, to love the solitary corner
Where he can patiently bear the weight of his poverty,
Forgetting that so many less worthy than he, like ravenous
  animals,
Gobble up the better part of everything,
Leaving him the pariah's bitter dregs.

And yet in poetry he always found not just beauty but spirit,
The strength to live with magnitude and freedom,

Como un neblí que deja el puño duro para buscar las nubes
Traslúcidas de oro allá en el cielo alto.
Ahora al reducto último de su casa y su huerto le alcanzan
  todavía
Las piedras de los otros, salpicaduras tristes
Del aguachirle caro para las gentes
Que forman el común y como público son árbitro de gloria.
Ni aun esto Dios le perdonó en la hora de su muerte.
Decretado es al fin que Góngora jamás fuera poeta,
Que amó lo oscuro y vanidad tan sólo le dictó sus versos.
Menéndez y Pelayo, el montañés henchido por sus dogmas,
No gustó de él y le condena con fallo inapelable.

Viva pues Góngora, puesto que así los otros
Con desdén le ignoraron, menosprecio
Tras del cual aparece su palabra encendida
Como estrella perdida en lo hondo de la noche,
Como metal insomne en las entrañas de la tierra.
Ventaja grande es que esté ya muerto
Y que de muerto cumpla los tres siglos, que así pueden
Los descendientes mismos de quienes le insultaban
Inclinarse a su nombre, dar premio al erudito,
Sucesor del gusano, royendo su memoria.
Mas el no transigió en la vida ni en la muerte
Y a salvo puso su alma irreductible
Como demonio arisco que ríe entre negruras.

Gracias demos a Dios por la paz de Góngora vencido;
Gracias demos a Dios por la paz de Góngora exaltado;
Gracias demos a Dios, que supo devolverle (como hará
  con nosotros),
Nulo al fin, ya tranquilo, entre su nada.

Like a falcon abandoning the clenched fist so he can soar
Into the gold rimmed clouds of the highest sky.
Now in the last redoubt of his home and garden,
Stones thrown by others keep on landing, splattering mud
Like cheap wine dear to the masses
Whose bad taste determines the fate of reputations.
God could not forgive him for this even as he was dying.
It is decreed in the end that Góngora was never a poet,
That he loved the obscure and that vanity alone fed him his lines.
Menéndez y Pelayo, the fat man from the highlands stuffed with
 dogma,
Disliked his work and handed down an unappealable verdict.

So long live Góngora, since that's the way others
Contemptuously dismissed him, a disdain
Through which his blazing language shines
Like a lost star in the depths of night,
Like a restless gem deep beneath the dirt.
To his great benefit he is now dead,
Three centuries gone, so that the offspring
Of the very ones who dismissed him
Can bow to his name and give prizes to the erudite
Descendants of the worms now feeding on his memory.
But he never compromised in life or in death
And protected his own indestructible soul
Like some surly devil laughing in the dark.

Thank God for the peace of defeated Góngora;
Thank God for the peace of exalted Góngora;
Thank God, who knew to return him (as he will us),
Nullified at last, becalmed, into nothingness.

Translator's note: Luis de Góngora (1561–1627), Baroque poet of the Golden Age, adopted by Cernuda's generation as a model of "impure poetry," had been discredited for some time in Spanish culture as an obscurantist literary anomaly, perhaps most definitively by Marcelino Menéndez y Pelayo (1856–1912), one of Spain's most eminent cultural historians and critics.

LA FAMILIA

¿Recuerdas tú, recuerdas aún la escena
A que día tras día asisiste paciente
En la niñez, remota como sueño al alba?
El silencio pesado, las cortinas caídas,
El círculo de luz sobre el mantel, solemne
Como paño de altar, y alrededor sentado
Aquel concilio familiar, que tantos ya cantaron,
Bien que tú, de entraña dura, aún no lo has hecho.

Era a la cabecera el padre adusto,
La madre caprichosa estaba en frente,
Con la hermana mayor imposible y desdichada,
Y la menor más dulce, quizá no más dichosa,
El hogar contigo mismo componiendo,
La casa familiar, el nido de los hombres,
Inconsistente y rígido, tal vidrio
Que todos quiebran, pero nadie dobla.

Presidían mudos, graves, la penumbra,
Ojos que no miraban los ojos de los otros,
Mientras sus manos pálidas alzaban como hostia
Un pedazo de pan, un fruto, una copa con agua,
Y aunque entonces vivían en ellos presentiste,
Tras la carne vestida, el doliente fantasma
Que al rezo de los otros nunca calma
La amargura de haber vivido inútilmente.

Suya no fue la culpa si te hicieron
En un rato de olvido indiferente,
Repitiendo tan sólo un gesto trasmitido
Por otros y copiado sin una urgencia propia,
Cuya intención y alcance no pensaban.

The Family

Remember, do you still remember the scene
Where you appeared patiently day after day
In childhood, as far away as a dream at dawn?
The heavy silence, the drapes drawn shut,
The circle of light above the tablecloth, solemn
As an altar, and seated around the table
The family council, a song sung by so many,
Even though you, with your hard head, never have.

At the head of the table the austere father,
Impulsive mother at the other end,
With the impossible and unhappy elder sister,
And the younger, sweeter one, perhaps no happier,
The household rounded out by you,
The family home, the human nest,
Thin and brittle as glass,
Which everyone breaks but no one bends.

Serious, silent, in a kind of twilight,
No one's eyes met anyone else's eyes,
While their pale hands lifted like the Host
A piece of bread, of fruit, a glass of water,
And though they were still alive you sensed in them,
Behind the well dressed flesh, the haunted pain
That all the prayers in the world could never relieve
The bitterness of having lived for nothing.

It wasn't their fault that they created you
In an ordinary moment of forgetting,
Merely going through the motions
Inherited from others, with no passion,
Whose purpose and implications they never thought of.

Tampoco fue tu culpa si no les comprendiste:
Al menos has tenido la fuerza de ser franco
Para con ellos y contigo mismo.

Se propusieron, como los hombres todos, lo durable,
Lo que les aprovecha, aunque en torno miren
Que nada dura en ellos ni aprovecha,
Que nada es suyo, ni ese trago de agua
Refrescando sus fauces en verano,
Ni la llama que templa sus manos, en invierno,
Ni el cuerpo que penetran con deseo
Dos soledades en una carne sola.

Ellos te dieron todo: cuando animal inerme
Te atendieron con leche y con abrigo;
Después, cuando creció tu cuerpo a par del alma,
Con dios y con moral te proveyeron,
Recibiendo deleite tras de azuzarte a veces
Para tu fuerza tierna doblegar a sus leyes.
Te dieron todo, si: vida que no pedías,
Y con ella la muerte de dura compañera.

Pero algo más había, agazapado
Dentro de ti, como alimaña en cueva oscura,
Que no te dieron ellos, y eso eres:
Fuerza de soledad, en ti pensarte vivo,
Ganando tu verdad con tus errores.
Así, tan libremente, el agua brota y corre,
Sin servidumbre de mover batanes,
Irreductible al mar, que es su destino.

Aquel amor de ellos te apresaba
Como prenda medida para otros,
Y aquella generosidad, que comprar pretendía
Tu asentimiento a cuanto

Nor was it your fault you couldn't understand them:
At least you had the courage to be honest
Both with them and with yourself.

What they proposed, like everyone else, was something
Lasting, what they had accomplished, though all around
They could see nothing lasts, nor is accomplished,
That nothing was theirs, not even that sip of water
Cooling their throats in summer,
Nor the flames warming their hands in winter,
Nor even the body joining in desire
Two solitudes in a single flesh.

They told you everything, how as a helpless baby
They gave you milk and swaddled you in warmth;
Later, when you grew into your own soul,
They provided you with morals and with God,
And sometimes it pleased you to arouse yourself
And prove your tender strength could break their laws.
They gave you everything, a life you never asked for
And with it death as a hard companion.

But there was something else, trapped
Inside you like a fox in a dark cave,
They never gave you, and that is what you are:
The strength of solitude, believing yourself alive,
Earning your own truth with your mistakes.
Water springs up like that and finds its way,
Free of the servitude of turning mills,
Downstream toward the sea, its destiny.

That love of theirs imprisoned you
Like a suit of clothes measured for someone else,
And that generosity that tried to buy
Your obedience in a way

No era según el alma tuya.
A odiar entonces aprendiste el amor que no sabe
Arder anónimo sin recompensa alguna.

El tiempo que pasó, desvaneciéndolos
Como burbuja sobre la haz del agua,
Rompió la pobre tiranía que levantaron,
Y libre al fin quedaste, a solas con tu vida,
Entre tantos de aquellos que, sin hogar ni gente,
Dueños en vida son del ancho olvido.

Luego con embeleso probando cuanto era
Costumbre suya prohibir en otros
Y a cuyo trasgresor la excomunión seguía,
Te acordaste de ellos, sonriendo apenado.
Cómo se engaña el hombre y cuán en vano
Da reglas que prohíben y condenan.
¿Es toda acción humana, como estimas ahora,
Fruto de imitación y de inconciencia?

Por esta extraña llama hoy trémula en tus manos,
Que aun deseándolo, temes ha de apagarse un día,
Hasta ti trasmitida con la herencia humana
De experiencias inútiles y empresas inestables
Obrando el bien y el mal sin proponérselo,
No prevalezcan las puertas del infierno
Sobre vosotros ni vuestras obras de la carne,
Oh padre taciturno que no le conociste,
Oh madre melancólica que no le comprendiste.

Que a esas sombras remotas no perturbe
En los limbos finales de la nada
Tu memoria como un remordimiento.
Este cónclave fantasmal que los evoca,

Your soul could not consent to.
And so you learned to hate the love that doesn't
Know how to burn unknown with no reward.

Time went by, undoing them
Like bubbles on the surface of a stream,
Dismantling the poor tyranny they'd built,
And leaving you free at last, alone with your life,
Like all the others with neither home nor kin,
Masters of their own oblivion.

Then when you had rapturously discovered
The way their customs are imposed on others
And how whoever breaks the rules is excommunicated,
You agreed with them, smiling through your pain.
How man deceives himself and how in vain
He makes laws that prohibit and condemn.
Is every human act, as you now believe,
No more than unthinking imitation?

For this strange flame now trembling in your hands,
Which you desire and fear will go out someday,
Come down to you as an inheritance
Of useless human experience, a shaky business
Toiling for good and ill without any meaning,
The gates of hell will not prevail
Over you nor your works of flesh and blood,
Oh taciturn father you never really knew,
Oh melancholy mother you never understood.

Don't let your memory trouble with remorse
Those distant shades now drifting out there
In the farthest reaches of nothingness.
May this ghostly conclave you've conjured up

Ofreciendo tu sangre tal bebida propicia
Para hacer a los idos visibles un momento,
Perdón y paz os traiga a ti y a ellos.

With your own blood like some magical drink
To make those lost ones visible for a moment
Bring peace and forgiveness to you all.

TARDE OSCURA

Lo mismo que un sueño
Al cuerpo separa
Del alma, esta niebla
Tierra y luz aparta.

Todo es raro y vago:
Ni són en el viento,
Latido en el agua,
Color en el suelo.

De sí mismo extraño,
¿Sabes lo que espera
El pájaro quieto
Por la rama seca?

Lejos, tras un vidrio,
Una luz ya arde,
Poniendo la hora
Más incierta. Yace

La vida, y tú solo,
No muerto, no vivo,
En el pecho sientes
Débil su latido.

Por estos suburbios
Sórdidos, sin norte
Vas, como el destino
Inútil del hombre.

Dark Afternoon

The same way a dream
Separates body
From soul, this fog
Divides land and light.

Everything's vague and strange:
No sound in the wind,
Rhythm in the water,
Color on the ground.

Estranged from itself,
Do you know what the quiet
Bird is waiting for
On the dry branch?

In the distance, behind a window,
A light is burning,
Making the hour seem
Still more uncertain. Life

Lies down, and you alone,
Neither dead nor living,
Can feel a faint heartbeat
Inside your chest.

You walk directionless
As human desiny
Through these squalid
Suburbs.

Y en el pensamiento
Luz o fe ahora
Buscas, mientras vence
Afuera la sombra.

And in your thought
You're looking for light
Or faith, while outside
Darkness conquers.

A UN POETA FUTURO

No conozco a los hombres. Años llevo
De buscarles y huirles sin remedio.
¿No les comprendo? ¿O acaso les comprendo
Demasiado? Antes que en estas formas
Evidentes, de brusca carne y hueso,
Súbitamente rotas por un resorte débil
Si alguien apasionado les allega,
Muertos en la leyenda les comprendo
Mejor. Y regreso de ellos a los vivos,
Fortalecido amigo solitario,
Como quien va del manantial latente
Al río que sin pulso desemboca.

No comprendo a los ríos. Con prisa errante pasan
Desde la fuente al mar, en ocio atareado,
Llenos de su importancia, bien fabril o agrícola;
La fuente, que es promesa, el mar sólo la cumple,
El multiforme mar, incierto y sempiterno.
Como en fuente lejana, en el futuro
Duermen las formas posibles de la vida
En un sueño sin sueños, nulas e inconscientes,
Prontas a reflejar la idea de los dioses.
Y entre los seres que serán un día
Sueñas tu sueño, mi imposible amigo.

No comprendo a los hombres. Mas algo en mí responde
Que te comprendería, lo mismo que comprendo
Los animales, las hojas y las piedras,
Compañeros de siempre silenciosos y fieles.
Todo es cuestión de tiempo en esta vida,
Un tiempo cuyo ritmo no se acuerda,
Por largo y vasto, al otro pobre ritmo
De nuestro tiempo humano corto y débil.

To a Future Poet

I'm mystified by men. For years now
I've been fruitlessly seeking and running away from them.
Mystified? Or maybe I understand them
All too well. Before they took these obvious
Flesh and blood forms
Easily broken by a weak spring
If they happen to meet a passionate person,
I understood them better in legend,
Dead. And I return from the dead to the living,
A fortified if solitary friend,
Like someone fresh from the headwaters
Flowing downriver freely into the sea.

I'm bewildered by rivers. In a wandering rush they flow
From the source to the ocean, working hard at being leisurely,
Full of themselves, running their farms and their factories;
The source is the promise, the ocean mere completion,
The shapeshifting ocean, uncertain and eternal.
As in faraway headwaters, life's potential future
Forms are fast asleep, in dreamless
Slumber, null and unconscious,
Soon to reveal the ideas of the gods.
And among those creatures to be someday
You, my impossible friend, are sleeping still.

I'm bewildered by men. But something in me knows
I would understand you, the same way I understand
Animals, leaves and stones,
Silent and ever faithful companions.
Everything's a matter of time in this life,
A time whose rhythm, as far back as it goes,
Is out of time with this other pitiful rhythm
Of our own brief and feeble human time.

Si el tiempo de los hombres y el tiempo de los dioses
Fuera uno, esta nota que en mí inaugura el ritmo,
Unida con la tuya se acordaría en cadencia,
No callando sin eco entre el mudo auditorio.

Mas no me cuido de ser desconocido
En medio de estos cuerpos casi contemporáneos,
Vivos de modo diferente al de mi cuerpo
De tierra loca que pugna por ser ala
Y alcanzar aquel muro del espacio
Separando mis años de los tuyos futuros.
Sólo quiero mi brazo sobre otro brazo amigo,
Que otros ojos compartan lo que miran los míos.
Aunque tú no sabrás con cuánto amor hoy busco
Por ese abismo blanco del tiempo venidero
La sombra de tu alma, para aprender de ella
A ordenar mi pasión según nueva medida.

Ahora, cuando me catalogan ya los hombres
Bajo sus clasificaciones y sus fechas,
Disgusto a unos por frío y a los otros por raro,
Y en mi temblor humano hallan reminiscencias
Muertas. Nunca han de comprender que si mi lengua
El mundo cantó un día, fue amor quien la inspiraba.
Ya no podré decirte cuánto llevo luchando
Para que mi palabra no se muera
Silenciosa conmigo, y vaya como un eco
A ti, como tormenta que ha pasado
Y un són vago recuerda por el aire tranquilo.

Tú no conocerás cómo domo mi miedo
Para hacer de mi voz mi valentía,
Dando al olvido inútiles desastres
Que pululan en torno y pisotean
Nuestra vida con estúpido gozo,
La vida que serás y que yo casi he sido.

If human time and the gods' time were the same,
This note that starts up a rhythm in me
Would find itself in harmony with yours,
Not silenced in some empty concert hall.

But I don't mind being unknown
Amid these near contemporary bodies
Alive in a different way than my body
Made of mad earth fighting to take flight
Over that wall of space and time
That separates my years from yours.
I want only to take a friend by the arm
And share with him whatever my eyes can see—
Though you can't know with how much love I'm looking
Across the blank void of time to come
In search of your soul's shadow, to learn from it
To set this passion of mine to a new measure.

Now, when people try to put me
In their stupid pigeonholes, some dislike me
For being cold and others for being strange,
And in my human heartbeat they find their own
Dead memories. They'll never understand that when my tongue
Sang of the world, it was inspired by love.
I can't tell you how long and hard I've fought
So that my words wouldn't die
Silently with me, and would go off
Like an echo in you, as after a storm,
A vague sound lingering in the calm air.

You'll never know how I mastered my fear
So I could turn my voice into my courage,
Tossing into oblivion those disasters
Swarming all around us, pointlessly,
Happily trampling our life,
The life you'll be and that I almost was.

Porque presiento en este alejamiento humano
Cuán míos habrán de ser los hombres venideros,
Cómo esta soledad será poblada un día,
Aunque sin mí, de camaradas puros a tu imagen.
Si renuncio a la vida es para hallarla luego
Conforme a mi deseo, en tu memoria.

Cuando en hora tardía, aún leyendo
Bajo la lámpara luego me interrumpo
Para escuchar la lluvia, pesada tal borracho
Que orina en la tiniebla helada de la calle,
Algo débil en mí susurra entonces:
Los elementos libres que aprisiona mi cuerpo
¿Fueron sobre la tierra convocados
Por esto sólo? ¿Hay más? Y si lo hay ¿adónde
Hallarlo? No conozco otro mundo si no es éste,
Y sin ti es triste a veces. Ámame con nostalgia,
Como a una sombra, como yo he amado
La verdad del poeta bajo nombres ya idos.

Cuando en días venideros, libre el hombre
Del mundo primitivo a que hemos vuelto
De tiniebla y de horror, lleve el destino
Tu mano hacia el volumen donde yazcan
Olvidados mis versos, y lo abras,
Yo sé que sentirás mi voz llegarte,
No de la letra vieja, mas del fondo
Vivo en tu entraña, con un afán sin nombre
Que tú dominarás. Escúchame y comprende.
En sus limbos mi alma quizá recuerde algo,
Y entonces en ti mismo mis sueños y deseos
Tendrá razón al fin, y habré vivido.

Because I sense in this estrangement from other people
How much like me some future men may be,
How full this solitude will be, without me,
Of loving comrades who look just like you.
If I renounce life it is only to find it later
In your memory of my desire.

When I'm up late, still reading
Under the lamp, and I take a break
To listen to the rain pouring down hard
Like a drunk pissing in the freezing street,
Some weak part of me whispers:
Were the free elements bound in my body
Gathered on earth for this
Alone? Isn't there anything else? And if so, where
Do I find it? This is the only world I know,
And without you, it's sad sometimes. Love me with nostalgia,
Like a shade, as I've loved names now gone
In the truth of their poems.

In days to come, when men are free
From the dark, horrible, primitive world
We've regressed to, destiny will guide
Your hand to this book where my lines
Lie forgotten, and you'll open it,
I know you'll feel my voice reaching out to you,
Not from the printed page but in the living
Depths of your being, with a passion you can't name
That you will master. Listen to me and understand.
In its netherworld my soul may remember something,
And then in you my dreams and desires will prove
True in the end, and I'll have lived.

APOLOGIA PRO VITA SUA

Abrid las puertas, dejad que vuelvan todos;
Su número es bien corto. Como en otro tiempo,
Espacio suficiente había para ellos
Adentro de mi amor; después ninguno ha entrado
Allá durante años. Igual es a una casa
Que el dueño olvida, ausente en otras tierras,
Donde nada interrumpe el gobernar oscuro
Del ratón, la polilla y telarañas,
Sino el rayo de sol, cuando penetra
Furtivo en el desván por un postigo hendido
Para agitar los sueños del polvo en formas grises;
O la rama de espino florido en primavera,
Contagiada del viento su locura,
Llamando persistente a los cristales, ciegos
Ante el albor perlado o la luna amarilla.

Dejadles que se acerquen a mi cama
Y alumbren sus semblantes, como estrellas
Suspensas en la noche sobre el agua oscura,
La agonía de aquel que les amara,
Uniéndoles así, desconocidos los unos a los otros,
En apretados haces de recuerdos.
Primero vienes tú, dame la mano, Arcángel,
Porque ya no conozco si te amaba o te odiaba,
Y perdón es ahora lo único que importa,
Antes de que a mi alma la destrone el olvido,
Cuyos pasos se acercan, rotos al fin muros y centinelas.
Si el amor no es un nombre, una experiencia inútil de los labios
(Así los dedos clavan un ala transparente
Tras el cristal curioso de algún laboratorio),
Yo creo que te he amado. Mas eso ya no importa.

Apologia pro Vita Sua

Open the doors and let them all come back;
There are few enough of them. Just as before,
There's plenty of room for them
Within my love; it's been years
Since anyone came in here. Like a house
Forgotten by its owner, absent in distant lands,
Where nothing interferes with the murky rule
Of the mice, the moths and the cobwebs
But a ray of sunlight slipping
Into the attic through a cracked shutter
To stir up the dreams of dusty gray forms;
Or a hawthorn blooming in springtime,
Its madness caught by the wind,
Insistently tapping at the windows
Blind to the pearly dawn or the yellow moon.

Let them come close to my bed
And their images illumine, like stars
Suspended in the night sky over dark water,
The agony of the one who loved them,
Bringing them together, unknown to one another,
In pressed bundles of memories.
You come first, give me your hand, Archangel,
Because I don't know anymore whether I loved or hated you,
And now all that matters is forgiveness
Before oblivion dethrones my soul,
Its footsteps approaching past all my shattered defenses.
If love is more than a word, a meaningless moving of lips
(The way fingers pin some transparent wing
Behind the curious glass of a laboratory),
I believe I loved you. But that's no longer important.

Deja pasar aquellos que ocuparon
Luego tu ausencia. Así al morir un rey
Otro ciñó la espada y la corona,
Sonando hacia la luna trompas en regocijo,
Aunque fuera excesivo para el nuevo monarca
El destino primero de aquel héroe,
Quien a sí mismo alzándose, alzó a sus sucesores
En el nombre, ya que no en la pasión dominadora.
¿No es la pasión medida de la grandeza humana
Y acero templado por su fuego el alma grande?
A mí esos otros cuerpos me enseñaron
Que si amor palidece, cuando ya es imposible
Creer en la verdad de quien se ama,
Crece aún el deseo, y vence con un fuego
Presagio de aquéllos en infierno ya sin esperanza.

Detrás venís vosotros, los amigos.
Qué dicen esos ojos aún claro lo recuerdo:
Si afuera es violento el mediodía,
Entra aquí. Facilidad sedante te brindamos;
Bodas de sombra y luz engendran la penumbra
Propicia a confidencias perezosas,
Y al nuevo visitante todo espera:
Asiento muelle, la copa con el vino,
Allá al rincón dormidas lilas blancas.
Benevolencia tibia le sienta bien al cuerpo
Que por desierto al sol ha caminado solo.
Después del purgatorio ¿no ha de ser grato el limbo?
Mas respeta la seña de esta hermandad, la tuya
Si a la pasión renuncias. Y nuestro olvido
Ha de vencer un día a tu memoria.

La razón era vuestra, mis amigos:
Es el olvido la verdad más alta.
De todos esos años ya pasados,
Llevándose mi vida, sólo quedan,

Let the ones who took the place
Of your absence come in. As when a king dies
Another puts on his sword and his crown,
Trumpets blowing at the moon in celebration,
Even though it were too much for the new monarch
To take on the destiny of that hero,
Who raising himself up raised his successors
In his name, if not in his ruling passion.
Is not passion the measure of human greatness
And the steel of the great soul tempered by its fire?
All those other bodies taught me
That if love fades away, when it's impossible
To believe in the truth of the one you love,
Desire still thrives and conquers with a fire
Foretelling the hopeless ones already in hell.

Behind them come you, friends.
What do those eyes say that I recall so clearly:
If the light of day is violent out there,
Come in here. Let's drink to your silken ease;
The marriage of light and darkness sheds a shadow
Just right for the sharing of leisurely secrets,
And everything awaits the new visitor:
A comfortable armchair, a glass of good wine,
Some white lilacs over in the corner.
Let his body feel a cool benevolence
After crossing the desert under the sun, alone.
Following purgatory, won't limbo feel good?
But accept the gesture of this brotherhood, yours
Once you've renounced all passion. And our oblivion
One day will obliterate your memory.

You were right, my friends:
Oblivion is the highest truth.
Of all those years gone by
Carrying off my life, all that remains,

Como cirio que arde en cueva oscura
Y mueve sombras vagas sobre el muro,
Recuerdos destinados a morir de mi olvido.
Yo los guardaba, como algunos guardan
Su amor, su ambición otros o su odio;
Valor, ninguno tienen. Y entre ellos,
Sueños brotados de las puertas córneas
Que amarga aquél brotado de puertas marfileñas,
Surgen dolientes esas sombras postreras:
Las sombras de la gente de mi sangre,
Clamando identidad que el alma desconoce.

Caminar a la muerte no es tan fácil,
Y si es duro vivir, morir tampoco es menos.
La llegada a esa meta final pudieron otros
Aliviarla, ya rota la cadena, el eslabón doliente
De la conciencia propia; no asistieron
Como yo insobornables al vencimiento amargo
De la muerte, renunciando a sus almas
Con adiós inconsciente. Yo contemplo
La mía, como pájaro herido bajo un ala
Que a tierra viene, mas lucha todavía
Con plumas abolidas que no sostiene el aire.
Cuán hermosa la luz parece ahora
Temblando en halo azul tras de las ramas
Pardas de invierno donde brilla el hielo.
La renuncia a la luz más que la muerte es dura.

Sólo resta decir: me pesan los pecados
Que la ocasión o fuerza de cometer no tuve.
He vivido sin ti, mi Dios, pues no ayudaste
Esta incredulidad que hizo triste mi alma.
Heme aquí ya vencido, presa fácil ahora
De tus ministros, cuyas manos alzadas
Remiten o condenan a los actos del hombre.
Pero ¿quién es el hombre para juzgar al hombre?

Like a candle burning in a dark cave
And casting murky shadows on the walls,
Are memories destined to die once I'm forgotten.
I clung to them, the way some cling
To their love, others their ambition or their hatred,
None of it worth anything. And among them,
Dreams sprung bitterly into existence
Through the ivory gates of my eyes,
Those final shadows surge up in pain:
Shadows of the people in my blood
Demanding recognition from a soul that doesn't know them.

Traveling into death is not so easy,
And if living is hard, dying is hardly less so.
Arrival at this point might have been alleviated
By others, but the chain is broken, the aching link
Of consciousness itself; they didn't fight
Like I did against death's bitter
Victory, they gave up their souls
With an unconscious goodbye. I think of mine
As a bird wounded under the wing
That crashes to the ground but keeps on struggling
With smashed feathers that have no lift.
How beautiful the light looks right now
Trembling in a blue haze behind winter's dark
Branches glazed with shining ice.
Giving up that light is even harder than dying.

All that's left to say is: I regret the sins
I never had the chance or the nerve to commit.
I've lived without you, God, because you could never
Relieve the disbelief that saddened my soul.
Here I am, defeated, easily imprisoned now
By your ministers, whose raised hands
Reward or condemn what men do.
But who is a man to judge a man?

La oración de la fe salva al enfermo,
Y si cayó en pecado le será perdonado.
Este cuerpo que ya sus elementos restituye
Al agua, al aire, al fuego y a la tierra,
Puede la gracia sellarlo todavía con un beso,
Por la virtud de aquel oscuro jugo de la oliva
Ungiendo al luchador y al moribundo.

Bien está que la sangre de la tierra
Moje y perdone al hombre cuando muere,
Aún turbias entreabriendo sus puertas los sentidos,
Y en ellas trace un dedo el signo mágico
Con el óleo más puro: sobre los ojos, que miraron
La luz y la hermosura, codiciándolas;
Sobre el oído, concha de la voz y la música;
Sobre el repliegue de la nariz, abierto
Al aroma del nardo, del cuerpo y de la lluvia;
Sobre la boca, que cantó, que besara y que mintiera;
Sobre la mano, de seda y de metales ambiciosa;
Sobre la espalda, árbol trémulo del espasmo.
Como un vuelo dibuja por el aire,
No la forma del ave, sino el surco efímero,
Desertan los recuerdos en nube mi memoria.

Para morir el hombre de Dios no necesita,
Mas Dios para vivir necesita del hombre.
Cuando yo muera, ¿el polvo dirá sus alabanzas?
Quien su verdad declare, ¿será el polvo?
Ida la imagen queda ciego el espejo.
No destruyas mi alma, oh Dios, si es obra de tus manos;
Sálvala con tu amor, donde no prevalezcan
En ella las tinieblas con su astucia profunda,
Y témplala con tu fuego hasta que pueda un día
Embeberse en la luz por ti creada.
Si dijiste, mi Dios, cómo ninguno
De los que en ti confíen ha de ser desolado,

A faithful prayer can save the one who's sick,
And if he sinned he'll be forgiven.
This body being reclaimed
By water, air, fire and earth
Can still be graced with the seal of a kiss,
The way the olive's dark green oil
Anoints both the fighter and the dying one.

It's a good thing the blood of the earth
Dampens and forgives a man when he's dying,
His senses still murkily half aware,
And that's where a finger must trace the magic sign
In the purest oil: on his eyes, which saw
Beauty and light, coveting them;
On his ears, shells echoing with music and voices;
On his nostrils, open
To the aromas of lilies, bodies and rain;
On his mouth, which sang, kissed and lied;
On his hands, greedy for jewels and silk;
On his back, a tree shaken with spasms.
Just as its flight sketches through the air
Not the bird's form but its fleeting wake,
My memory is vanishing into the clouds.

Man needs no God to help him die,
But in order to live, God needs man.
When I die, will the dust celebrate me?
Who will tell the truth, only the dust?
Once the image is gone, the mirror is blind.
God, don't destroy my soul, if it's your creation;
Save it with your love, where darkness
And its deep insight can't prevail,
And temper it with your fire until one day
It is consumed by the light you created.
If you would only say, my God, that none
Who put their faith in you will be abandoned,

Tras esta noche oscura vendrá el alba
Y hallaremos en ti resurrección y vida.
Para que entre la luz abrid las puertas.

After this long dark night daylight will come
And in you we will find life and resurrection.
Open the doors and let the light come in.

Translator's note: Cernuda titles this faithless "deathbed" poem after the 1864 essay by John Henry Newman in defense of his Catholic faith.

PRIMAVERA VIEJA

Ahora, al poniente morado de la tarde,
En flor ya los magnolios mojados de rocío,
Pasar aquellas calles, mientras crece
La luna por el aire, será soñar despierto.

El cielo con su queja harán más vasto
Bandos de golondrinas; el agua en una fuente
Librará puramente la honda voz de la tierra;
Luego el cielo y la tierra quedarán silenciosos.

En el rincón de algún compás, a solas
Con la frente en la mano, un fantasma
Que vuelve, llorarías pensando
Cuán bella fue la vida y cuán inútil.

A Springtime Long Ago

Now in the purple light of a sunken sun,
The flowering magnolias damp with dew,
To walk along those streets as the full moon
Rises in the sky is a waking dream.

The swallows with their cries filling the sky
Make it seem even vaster; a gurgling fountain
Freely releases the pure deep voice of the earth;
Then sky and earth alike return to silence.

In a corner of some courtyard, all alone
With head in hand, a ghost who has come home,
You would be weeping now, weeping and thinking
How beautiful this life was, and how useless.

QUETZALCÓATL

Yo estaba allí, mas no me preguntéis
De dónde o cómo vino, sabed sólo
Que estuve yo también cuando el milagro.
No importa el nombre. Una aldea cualquiera
Me vio nacer allá en el mundo viejo
Y apenas vivo me adiestré en la vida
Del miserable: hambre, frío, trabajo
Con soledad. ¿Quién le dio al fango un alma?

Pero tuve algo más: el cielo aquel, el cielo
De la tarde en Castilla (puro y vasto
Como frente de un dios que piensa el mundo,
Un mar de sangre y oro, cuya fiebre
La calmaba, toda azul, la noche honda
Con su perenne escalofrío de estrellas),
Me enseñó la lección digna del alma
Cuando lo contemplaba yo de niño
Sobre las bardas últimas al páramo.

Luego, como arenal sediento bebe el agua,
Así embebió mi mente las leyendas
De aquellos que pasaban a las Indias,
Perla sin par oculta en el abismo atlántico
Y por un hombre hallada, para adornar con ella,
Poeta que regala su propio sueño vivo,
Manos regias avaras y crueles.

Cuando vi un día las murallas rojas
De la costa alejarse, y yo perderme
En la masa de agua, sentí ceder el nudo
Que invisible nos ata a nuestra tierra;
Madrastra fuera, que no madre, y aún la quise.

Quetzalcóatl

I was there, but don't ask
From where or how I came, know only
That I too witnessed the miracle.
My name doesn't matter. I could have been born
In any village back in the old world
And from the start I was trained in the life
Of the miserable: hunger, cold, solitary
Labor. Who was it that cast a soul into the mire?

But I had something more: that sky, the sky
Of the Castilian afternoon (vast and clear
As a god's face thinking up the world,
An ocean of blood and gold, whose fever
Calmed the deep blue night
With its always shivering stars),
Taught me a lesson worthy of the soul
When as a boy I watched it
Above the thatched roofs at the edge of the wildlands.

Later, the way a thirsty desert soaks up water,
My mind drank in the legends
Of the men who traveled to the Indies,
Those incomparable pearls hidden in the bottomless Atlantic
And discovered by a man, a poet who gives
His living dream as a gift to adorn
The cruel and greedy hands of kings and queens.

When one day I saw the red cliffs
Of the coast growing distant, and myself being lost
On the vast waters, I felt the knot that binds us
Invisibly to our land loosening;
It was a stepmother, not my mother, yet I loved her.

Comencé entonces a morir, mas era joven
Y en ello no pensé, dándolo al olvido.
Otras constelaciones velaron mi esperanza.

Pisando tierra nueva, de la mano el destino
Me llevó llanamente al hombre designado
Para la hazaña: aquel Cortés, demonio o ángel,
Como queráis; para mí sólo un hombre
Tal manda Dios, apasionado y duro,
Temple de diamante, que es fuego congelado
A cuya vista ciega quien le mira.

La ciudad contemplada desde el monte
Desnuda la intención secreta de sus calles,
Creídas al pisarla confusión sin rumbo;
Así desnudó el tiempo aquellos años nuestros
Preliminares, aunque perdidos parecieran:
Su dispersión impulsó al aire la semilla
Que caída en la tierra dio luego la cosecha.

Y el momento llegó cuando nos fuimos
Por el mar un puñado de hombres;
El mundo era sin límite, igual a mi deseo.
Frente al afán de ver, de ver con estos ojos
Que ha de cegar la muerte, lo demás, ¿qué valía?
Mas este pensamiento a nadie dije
Entre mis compañeros, a quienes hostigaba
La ambición de riqueza y poderío.

Realidad fabulosa como leyenda alguna
Allá nos esperaba, y nosotros la hallamos
Tras sus cimas nevadas y sus lagos profundos:
Un reino virgen cimentado en el oro y la esmeralda,
Guardado por cobrizas criaturas recónditas
Para las cuales Cristo fue nombre nunca oído.

That's when I started to die, but I was young
And didn't give it a thought, I forgot about it.
My hopes were guided by other constellations.

Once on the new land, destiny bound me
Plainly to the man it chose
For the deed: Cortés, devil or angel,
As you prefer; to me just a man
Commanded by God, passionate, tough,
Hard as a diamond, whose frozen fire
Blinds whoever looks into its light.

The city we saw from the mountains
Revealed the secret plan of its streets,
Believed to bewilder whoever entered;
That's how time stripped bare those early years
Of ours, though they may have appeared aimless:
Their scatterings launched the seeds
That fell on earth and later yielded the harvest.

And the moment came when a handful of men
Took to the sea;
The world was limitless, like my desire.
Faced with the passion for seeing, seeing with these eyes
That death would someday blind, what was the rest worth?
But I spoke this thought to none
Of my companions, who were driven
By their ambition for power and riches.

A reality as fabulous as any legend
Was waiting for us there, and we found it
Beyond its snowy peaks and bottomless lakes:
A virgin kingdom studded with gold and emeralds,
Guarded by coppery inscrutable creatures
Who had never heard the name of Christ.

Astucia, fuerza, crueldad y crimen,
Todo lo cometimos, y nos fue devuelto
Con creces; mas vencimos, y nadie hizo otro tanto
Antes, ni hará después: un puñado de hombres
Que la codicia apenas guardó unidos
Ganaron un imperio milenario.

Ya sé lo que decís: el horror de la guerra,
Mas lo decís en paz, y en guerra calláis con mansedumbre.
Nadie supo la guerra tan bien como nosotros,
Ni siquiera los hombres allá en el mundo viejo
Donde el emperador un trozo de pan daba
Por conquistarle reinos: castillos en el aire,
No bien ganados cuando ya perdidos.

Cuerpos acometí, arrancando sus almas
Apenas fatigadas de la vida,
Como el aire inconsciente las hojas de una rama;
Destinos corté en flor, por la corola
Aún intacto el color, puro el perfume.
¿Hubo algún Garcilaso que mi piedra
Hundiera bruscamente al fondo de la muerte?
El reino del poeta tampoco es de este mundo.

Cuando en una mañana, por los arcos y puertas
Que abrió la capital vencida ante nosotros,
Onduló como serpiente de bronce y diamante
Cortejo con litera trayendo al rey azteca,
Me pareció romperse el velo mismo
De los últimos cielos, desnuda ya la gloria.
Sí, allí estuve, y lo vi; envidiadme vosotros.

La masa nevada de terrazas y torres,
Por la ciudad lejana de innumerables puentes,
Se copiaba en el agua áurea de las lagunas

Cunning, brute force, cruelty and crime,
We did it all, and it came back to us
With interest; but we overcame, and no one
Had done that before, nor has done it since:
A handful of men barely united by greed
Won for themselves a millenarian empire.

I know what you're saying: the horror of war,
But you say it in peacetime, and in war your were meekly
silenced.
No one else knew war as well as we did,
Not even those men back there in the old world
Where the emperor conquered kingdoms
With a piece of bread: castles in the air,
Scarcely won and just as quickly lost.

I attacked bodies, ripping out souls
That weren't yet tired of living
As the unconscious wind strips leaves from a branch;
I cut short destinies in bloom, the color still bright
In their corollas, their scent still pure.
Was there a Garcilaso whom my blow
Sent abruptly to the depths of death?
Nor is the poet's kingdom of this world.

When one morning a serpent of bronze and diamonds
Came undulating through the gates and arches of the capital
We had taken, the cortege
With the litter bearing the Aztec king,
The very veil of the last skies seemed to tear
Revealing glory in its nakedness.
Yes, I was there, I saw it; envy me.

The snowy mass of terraces and towers
Across the distant city of countless bridges,
Was mirrored in the golden waters of the lagoons

Como sueño esculpido en luz gloriosa,
Y encima refulgía la corona del cielo.

Pobre rey Moctezuma, golondrina
Rezagada que sorprende el invierno,
Mojada y aterida el ala ya sin fuerza.
Pero no es rey quien nace, y Cortés lo sabía.
¿Por qué lo olvidó luego, emulando con duques
En la corte lejana, él, cuyos pies se hicieron
Para besarlos príncipes y reyes?
Cuando él se abandonó también Dios le abandona.

Ahora amigos y enemigos están muertos
Y yace en paz el polvo de unos y de otros,
Menos yo: en mi existencia juntas sobreviven
Victorias y derrotas que el recuerdo hizo amigas.
¿Quién venció a quién?, a veces me pregunto.

Nada queda hoy que hacer, acotada la tierra
Que ahora el traficante reclama como suya
Negociando con cuerpos y con almas;
Ya sólo puede el hombre hacer dinero o hijos.
Y en un rincón al sol de este suelo, más mío
Que lo es el otro allá en el mundo viejo, solo, pobre
Tal vine, aguardo el fin sin temor y sin prisa.

Del viento nació el dios y volvió al viento
Que hizo de mí una pluma entre sus alas.
Oh tierra de la muerte, ¿dónde está tu victoria?

Like a dream sculpted in glorious light,
And above it all the shining crown of the sky.

Poor King Montezuma, a lingering
Swallow surprised by winter,
Its wings now wet and cold and without strength.
But no man born is a king, and Cortés knew it.
Why did he later forget it, emulating dukes
In the faraway court—he, whose feet were made
To be kissed by kings and princes?
When he abandoned himself, God too abandoned him.

Now the friends and the enemies are dead
And the dust of the ones and the others rests in peace,
Except for me: in my existence victories and defeats
Survive together, made friends in memory.
Who conquered whom? I sometimes ask myself.

There's nothing left to be done, the earth is all staked out
By businessmen who claim it as their own,
Wheeling and dealing in bodies and souls;
Now a man can make only money or children.
And in a corner under the sun of this land, more mine
Than the other one in the old world, alone, poor
As I came, I await the end at leisure, fearing nothing.

The god who made me a feather in his wings
Was born of the wind and is gone with the wind.
Oh land of death, where is your victory?

Translator's note: Quetzalcóatl, the mythical plumed serpent of Aztec prophecy, was identified with the arrival in Mexico of Hernán Cortés and his band of Spanish conquerors in 1519. The speaker of this poem, an Ishmael-like survivor, is one of these soldiers. Cernuda didn't know, at the time this poem was written, that he too would spend his final years in Mexico.

LOS ESPINOS

Verdor nuevo los espinos
Tienen ya por la colina,
Toda de púrpura y nieve
En el aire estremecida.

Cuántos ciclos florecidos
Les has visto; aunque a la cita
Ellos serán siempre fieles,
Tú no lo serás un día.

Antes que la sombra caiga,
Aprende cómo es la dicha
Ante los espinos blancos
Y rojos en flor. Vé. Mira.

Hawthorns

The hawthorns on the hillside now
Are gleaming a fresh green
All tipped with purple and with snow
Shimmering in the sun.

How many flowering cycles of time
You've seen them; and even though
They faithfully keep every date,
One of these days you won't.

And so before the darkness falls,
Learn what happiness is
Just looking, seeing the hawthorns
In flower, white and red.

ELEGÍA ANTICIPADA

Por la costa del sur, sobre una roca
Alta junto a la mar, el cementerio
Aquel descansa en codiciable olvido,
Y el agua arrulla el sueño del pasado.

Desde el dintel, cerrado entre los muros,
Huerto parecería, si no fuese
Por las losas, posadas en la hierba
Como un poco de nieve que no oprime.

Hay troncos a que asisten fuerza y gracia,
Y entre el aire y las hojas buscan nido
Pájaros a la sombra de la muerte;
Hay paz contemplativa, calma entera.

Si el deseo de alguien, que en el tiempo
Dócil no halló la vida sus deseos,
Puede cumplirse luego, tras la muerte,
Quieres estar allá solo y tranquilo.

Ardido el cuerpo, luego lo que es aire
Al aire vaya, y a la tierra el polvo,
Por obra del afecto de un amigo,
Si un amigo tuviste entre los hombres.

Y no es el silencio solamente,
La quietud del lugar, quien así lleva
Tu memoria hacia allá, mas la conciencia
De que tu vida allí tuvo su cima.

Fue en la estación cuando la mar y el cielo
Dan una misma luz, la flor es fruto,

Elegy in Advance

On the southern coast, on a high
Cliff above the sea, that cemetery
Rests enviably unremembered,
And the surf murmurs dreamily of the past.

From the gateway, shut between walls,
You'd think it was a garden, if it weren't
For the gravestones, poised on the grass
Like a light dusting of snow.

The trunks of trees contribute strength and grace,
And in the airy leaves above, birds look
For a place to build their nest in the shade of death;
A completely calm, contemplative peace prevails.

If someone's desire was not fulfilled
In the course of a lifetime,
Later it can be, after death,
You just need to be there, quiet and alone.

Your body burned, then what is air
May join the air, and dust the earth,
Thanks to the affection of a friend,
If among men you ever had a friend.

And it isn't just the silence,
The stillness of the place, that takes
Your memory there, but the knowledge
That here you reached the summit of your life.

It was the time of year when sea and sky
Reflect each other's light, and buds bear fruit,

Y el destino tan pleno que parece
Cosa dulce adentrarse por la muerte.

Entonces el amor único quiso
En cuerpo amanecido sonreírte,
Esbelto y rubio como espiga al viento.
Tú mirabas tu dicha sin creerla.

Cuando su cetro el día pasa luego
A su amada la noche, aún más hermosa
Parece aquella tierra; un dios acaso
Vela en eternidad sobre su sueño.

Entre las hojas fuisteis, descuidados
De una presencia intrusa, y ciegamente
Un labio hallaba en otro ese embeleso
Hijo de la sonrisa y del suspiro.

Al alba el mar pulía vuestros cuerpos,
Puros aún, como de piedra oscura;
La música a la noche acariciaba
Vuestras almas debajo de aquel chopo.

No fue breve esa dicha. ¿Quién pretende
Que la dicha se mida por el tiempo?
Libres vosotros del espacio humano,
Del tiempo quebrantasteis las prisiones.

El recuerdo por eso vuelve hoy
Al cementerio aquel, al mar, la roca
En la costa del sur: el hombre quiere
Caer donde el amor fue suyo un día.

And destiny has been so kind to you
That entering death feels like a sweet fulfillment.

That's when new love wanted only
To smile at you in an awakening body,
Slender and blond like a wheat stalk in the breeze.
You were looking at luck you could scarcely believe.

When daylight hands its scepter over
To its lover, night, that land looks
Even more lovely; perhaps some god
In eternity is watching over its sleep.

You walked beneath those leaves, not caring
That you were intruders, and blindly
One mouth found in another the rapture
That mates a sigh with a smile.

At dawn the ocean polished your bodies,
Still pure, as if made of dark rock;
The sound of its nightlong music caressed
Your souls beneath that poplar.

That happiness wasn't brief. Who claims
Such joy can be measured in time?
Free from the prison of human space
You'd broken out of time's walls.

That's why your memory now returns
To that cemetery, that sea, that cliff
On the southern coast: a man wants
To fall where one day love was his.

APLAUSO HUMANO

Ahora todas aquellas criaturas grises
Cuya sed parca de amor nocturnamente satisface
El aguachirle conyugal, al escuchar tus versos,
Por la verdad que exponen podrán escarnecerte.

Cuánto pedante en moda y periodista en venta
Humana flor perfecta se estimarán entonces
Frente a ti, así como el patán rudimentario
Hasta la náusea hozando la escoria del deseo.

La consideración mundana tú nunca la buscaste,
Aún menos cuando fuera su precio una mentira,
Como bufón sombrío traicionado tu alma
A cambio de un cumplido con oficial benevolencia.

Por ello en vida y muerte pagarás largamente
La ocasión de ser fiel contigo y unos pocos,
Aunque jamás sepan los otros que desvío
Siempre es razón mejor ante la grey.

Pero a veces aún dudas si la verdad del alma
No debiera guardarla el alma a solas,
Contemplarla en silencio, y así nutrir la vida
Con un tesoro intacto que no profana el mundo.

Mas tus labios hablaron, y su verdad fue al aire.
Sigue con la frente tranquila entre los hombres,
Y si un sarcasmo escuchas, súbito como piedra,
Formas amargas del elogio ahí descifre tu orgullo.

Human Praise

Now when they hear your poems
All those grayish creatures whose pitiful thirst
For love is satisfied by their watery conjugal cocktail
Can laugh at you for having told the truth.

See how the professor à la mode and the hack reviewer
Compared to you will feel themselves the perfect
Flowering of humanity, like pigs
Rooting through whatever's left of desire.

You never sought their pedestrian attention,
Even less when you would have had to lie,
Like some gloomy fool betraying your own soul
To kiss the official buttocks of the times.

That's why in life and death you will pay dearly
For having stayed true to yourself and a few friends,
Even though the others will never know
How right you were to break away from the herd.

And yet sometimes you wonder whether the soul
Shouldn't just keep its truth to itself,
Quietly contemplating, nurturing life
With an untouched treasure the world will never spoil.

But your lips spoke, and your truth escaped,
So carry on calmly through the world of men,
And if you hear a snide comment tossed like a rock,
Let your pride find that a bitter form of praise.

OTROS TULIPANES AMARILLOS

Primavera con niebla, amarga, sin perfume,
De verde y gris tan vago tal si el halo
De plata que la envuelve luz no fuera,
Mas sueño; deshecha en lluvia leve
Moja hierba y piedra, sobre la tierra anima
Tulipanes dorados, cuyo color tan vivo
Es como son perdido por el aire sordo.

¿Dónde recuerdas tú de otra primavera,
En otra tierra y tiempo, mojada como ésta
Con lluvia leve, como ésta cifrada
En otros tulipanes amarillos?
Entonces algo más florecía, aunque no en tierra;
En ti. Tanta luz amarilla duele ahora,
O ¿no será el recuerdo lo que duele?

Es cruel la primavera joven, precipita
Al hombre por el viejo camino de los yerros,
Con ramas de cerezo florido lo enajena,
Con viento del sur tibio lo extravía.
Mas esta que tu pecho inerme siempre
Toca ahora como el ala un vidrio,
No te seduce ya con presagios ilusorios,
Sino con unos ecos, con algunos recuerdos.

Así te vuelve hoy aquella sombra
Lejana, que por una lejana primavera,
También gris y amarilla, quiso amarte
Con capricho egoísta, como el hombre ama
En un mundo incompleto (y aún es mucho);
A quien la mano de la muerte puso en fuga
Como la mano nuestra en fuga pone al pájaro.

Some Other Yellow Tulips

A foggy, bitter spring, with no perfume,
With greens and grays so empty that the silvery
Halo enveloping them is less light
Than a dream; dissolved in drizzle,
The grass and stones are damp, and on the land
Golden tulips whose color is so alive
It's like a sound lost in the deaf air.

From where do you recall that other spring,
In another land and time, damp like this
With drizzle, and spelling itself out
In other yellow tulips?
Something else bloomed then, though not from the earth;
In you. Now so much yellow light hurts,
Or maybe it's the memory that aches.

Young spring is cruel, it drives
A man down the old roads of his mistakes,
Feeling estranged from the cherry trees in bloom,
Disoriented by the warm breeze from the south.
Yet this thing touching your always unarmed heart
The way a bird's wing taps at a windowpane
Doesn't seduce you now with illusory visions,
But with a few echoes, a few recollections.

That's how that distant darkness returns
To you now, as if a distant springtime,
Also gray and yellow, were seducing you
Capriciously, selfishly, the way a man makes love
In an incomplete world (which is still too much);
A man in flight from the hand of death
The same way our hand puts birds in flight.

Nuestra vida parece que está aquí: con hojas
Seguras en su rama, hasta que nazca el frío;
Con flores en su tallo, hasta que brote el viento;
Con luz allá en su cielo, hasta que surjan nubes.
Tal vez por un momento cierto te creyeras
En el mundo del hombre, si no fuese
Por aquel otro mundo de las sombras
Que al cuerpo lo consume como a luna menguante.

¿Qué empresa nuestra es ésta, abandonada
Inútilmente un día? ¿Qué afectos imperiosos
Éstos, con cuyos nombres se alimenta el olvido?
Ya en tu vida las sombras pesan más que los cuerpos;
Llámalos hoy, si hay alguno que escuche
Entre la hierba sola de esta primavera,
Y aprende ese silencio antes que el tiempo llegue.

Our life appears to be here: with leaves
Fixed to their branches until the cold comes;
With flowers on their stems, until the wind picks up;
With light in the sky, until the clouds roll down.
Maybe for a minute you could have believed
In the human world, if it weren't
For that other world of the dark
Devouring your body like a waning moon.

What is this business of ours, discarded
One day, pointlessly? What are these urgent
Feelings, whose names oblivion feeds on?
By now in your life the shades outweigh the bodies;
Call them, just in case one may be listening
Out in the lonely grasses of this spring,
And come to know that silence while you can.

EL INDOLENTE

Con hombres como tú el comercio sería
Cosa leve y tan pura que, sin sudor ni sangre
De ninguno comprada, dejaría a la tierra
Intactos sus veneros. Pero a tu pobreza
El comercio podría allanarle un camino.

Durante las tardes meridionales del verano,
A través de una clara ciudad, solas las calles,
Llevarías en cestillo guirnaldas de jazmines,
Y magnolias, por un nido fragante de hojas verdes
Oculto su blancor, como alas de paloma.

Tras de las rejas bajas, si una mujer quisiera
Para su gracia oscura tal vez la fresca gala
De una flor, y prenderla en su pelo o en su pecho,
Donde ha de parecer nieve sobre la tierra,
Una moneda a cambio dejaría en tus manos.

Así, al ponerse la tarde, tú podrías
De un vino transparente beber el calor rubio,
Mordiendo la delicia de un pan y de una fruta,
Y luego silencioso, tendido junto al río,
Ver latir en la honda noche las estrellas.

The Lazy Man

For men like you, your line of work would be
A light, pure thing, bought without anyone's
Blood or sweat, that would leave the springs
Of the earth unspoiled. But this business
Would clear you a smooth path to your poverty.

Under the high sun of summer afternoons,
Across a bright city, alone through the streets,
You'd carry a basket of jasmine flowers
And sweet magnolias covered with leaves,
Their whiteness hidden, like the wings of doves.

From behind a low railing, if a woman wanted
A fresh corsage to accent her dark beauty,
And fasten it in her hair or between her breasts,
Where it would look like snow against the earth,
In exchange she'd drop a coin into your hand.

And that's how, at day's end, you'd be able to drink
The sun's blond warmth in a glass of good wine,
And savor a bite of bread, a piece of fruit,
And then very quietly, lying by the river, look up
At the stars throbbing deep in the dark night.

NOCHE DEL HOMBRE Y SU DEMONIO

D: Vive la madrugada. Cobra tu señorío.
Percibe la existencia en dolor puro.
Ahora el alma es oscura, y los ojos no hallan
Sino tiniebla en torno. Es ésta la hora cierta
Para hablar de la vida, la vida tan amada.
Si al Dios de quien es obra le reprochas
Que te la diera limitada en muerte,
Su don en sueños no malgastes. Hombre, despierta.

H: Entre los brazos de mi sueño estaba
Aprendiendo a morir. ¿Por qué me acuerdas?
¿Te inspira acaso envidia el sueño humano?
Amo más que la vida este sosiego a solas,
Y tú me arrancas de él, para volverme
Al carnaval de sombras, por el cual te deslizas
Con ademán profético y paso insinuante
Tal ministro en desgracia no quiero verte. Déjame.

D: No sólo forja el hombre a imagen propia
Su Dios, aún más se le asemeja su demonio.
Acaso mi apariencia no concierte
Con mi poder latente: aprendo hipocresía,
Envejezco además, y ya desmaya el tiempo
El huracán sulfúreo de las alas
En el cuerpo del ángel que fui un día.
En mí tienes espejo. Hoy no puedo volverte
La juventud huraña que de ti ha desertado.

H: En la hora feliz del hombre, cuando olvida,
Aguzas mi conciencia, mi tormento;
Como enjambre irritado los recuerdos atraes;
Con sarcasmo mundano suspendes todo acto,
Dejándolo incompleto, nulo para la historia,

Night of a Man and His Demon

D: The hours before dawn are alive. They rule your realm.
They understand the pure grief of existence.
Your soul is in the dark now, and your eyes find nothing
But darkness around you. This is the right time
To talk about life, the life you love so much.
If you blame God, whose creation it is,
For giving it to you wrapped in death,
Don't waste his gift on dreaming. Wake up, man.

M: In my sleep's embrace I was
Learning to die. Why remind me?
Maybe you envy a man his dreams?
I love this solitary break even more than living,
And you uproot me from it to drag me back
To the carnival of shadows you've slipped out of
With a prophet's attitude and the smooth moves
Of a disgraced diplomat. Get out of here. Leave me alone.

D: A man's not the only thing forged in God's image;
His demon bears an even stronger resemblance.
Maybe my appearance fails to suggest
My hidden powers: I know hypocrisy,
I get old besides, and the sulfuric hurricane
Of wings on the body of the angel I once was
Makes time faint.
I'm your mirror. I can't give back
The fleeting youth that has deserted you.

M: In a man's happiest hours, when he's forgetting,
You prod my consciousness, my suffering;
You stir up memories like a swarm of hornets;
Your sarcasm sabotages every deed,
Leaving it undone and come to nothing,

Y luego, comparando cuánto valen
Ante un chopo con sol en primavera
Los sueños del poeta, susurras cómo el sueño
Es de esta realidad la sombra inútil.

D: Tu inteligencia se abre entre el engaño:
Es como flor a un viejo regalada,
Y a poco que la muerte se demore,
Ella será clarividente un día.
Mas si el tiempo destruye la sustancia,
Que aquilate la esencia ya no importa.
Ha sido la palabra tu enemigo:
Por ella de estar vivo te olvidaste.

H: Hoy me reprochas el culto a la palabra.
¿Quién si no tú puso en mí esa locura?
El amargo placer de transformar el gesto
En són, sustituyendo el verbo al acto,
Ha sido afán constante de mi vida.
Y mi voz no escuchada, o apenas escuchada,
Ha de sonar aún cuando yo muera,
Sola, como el viento en los juncos sobre el agua.

D: Nadie escucha una voz, tú bien lo sabes.
¿Quién escuchó jamás la voz ajena
Si es pura y está sola? El histrión elocuente,
El hierofante vano miran crecer el corro
Propicio a la mentira. Ellos viven, prosperan;
Tú vegetas sin nadie. El mañana ¿qué importa?
Cuando a ellos les olvide el destino, y te recuerde,
Un nombre tú serás, un són, un aire.

H: Me hieres en el centro más profundo,
Pues conoces que el hombre no tolera
Estar vivo sin más: como en un juego trágico
Necesita apostar su vida en algo,

And then, weighing the value
Of a poet's dreams against a poplar in spring sun,
You whisper that dreams
Are a worthless shadow of that reality.

D: Your intelligence is born of an illusion:
It's like a flower given to an old man,
And if that seems to delay death for a while,
Soon enough it will all come clear.
But if time wipes out material things,
The value of essences counts for nothing.
Language has been your enemy:
Because of it you forgot to be alive.

M: Now you blame me for believing in words.
Was it anyone but you who filled me with this madness?
The bitter pleasure of turning actions
Into sounds, of replacing deeds with words,
Has been the constant passion of my life.
And my voice, scarcely heard now, or not at all,
Will go on sounding after I'm dead,
All by itself, like wind in the reeds by the river.

D: Nobody hears one voice, you know that much.
Who ever heard a single stranger's voice
That's pure and solitary? The charlatan,
The cocky preacher watch their followings grow
Fed on their lies. They live, they prosper;
You slowly rot, alone. What does tomorrow matter?
When destiny forgets them, and you're remembered,
You'll be a name, a sound, a breath of air.

M: You twist your knife in the deepest part of me,
You know no man can tolerate being
Merely alive: as in some tragic game
He has to stake his life on something,

Algo de que alza un ídolo, aunque con barro sea,
Y antes que confesar su engaño quiere muerte.
Mi engaño era inocente, y nadie arruinaba
Excepto a mí, aunque a veces yo mismo lo veía.

D: Siento esta noche nostalgia de otras vidas.
Quisiera ser el hombre común de alma letárgica
Que extrae de la moneda beneficio,
Deja semilla en la mujer legítima,
Sumisión cosechando con la prole,
Por pública opinión ordena su conciencia
Y espera en Dios, pues frecuentó su templo.

H: ¿Por qué de mí haces burla duramente?
Si pierde su sabor la sal del mundo
Nada podrá volvérselo, y tú no existirías
Si yo fuese otro hombre más feliz acaso,
Bien que no es la cuestión el ser dichoso.
Amo el sabor amargo y puro de la vida,
Este sentir por otros la conciencia
Aletargada en ellos, con su remordimiento,
Y aceptar los pecados que ellos mismos rechazan.

D: Pobre asceta irrisorio, confiesa cuánto halago
Ofrecen el poder y la fortuna:
Alas para cernerse al sol, negar la zona
En sombra de la vida, gratificar deseos,
Con dúctil amistad verse fortalecido,
Comprarlo todo, ya que todo está en venta,
Y contemplando la miseria extraña
Hacer más delicado el placer propio.

H: Dos veces no se nace, amigo. Vivo al gusto
De Dios. ¿Quién evadió jamás a su destino?
El mío fue explorar esta extraña comarca,
Contigo siempre a zaga, subrayando

Something to idolize, if only a clay statue,
And he'd rather die than admit he's been tricked.
My mistake was innocent, and it ruined no one
But me, though at times even I could see right through it.

D: I'm feeling nostalgic tonight for other lives.
I'd like to be an ordinary man with a slack soul
Who gains some benefit from money,
Leaves his seed inside his lawful wife,
Reaps the obedience of his offspring,
Shapes his thinking according to public opinion,
Believes in God and weekly goes to his church.

M: Why are you giving me such a hard time?
If the salt of the earth has lost its taste
Nothing can bring it back, and you wouldn't even exist
If I were someone else and maybe a little happier,
Not that it's a question of being happy.
I love the pure, bitter flavor of life,
This feeling for others a consciousness
They've lost, with its regrets,
And accepting the sins they themselves have rejected.

D: You poor joke of a monk, admit what privileges
The rich and the powerful reap:
Wings that can sift sunlight, deny
The dark side of life, gratify desires;
They fortify themselves with comforting friendships,
Can buy anything, since everything's for sale,
And contemplating the misery of others
Feel their pleasures to be even sweeter.

M: We're not born twice, my friend. I live at the pleasure
Of God. Who ever escaped his destiny?
Mine was to explore this strange terrain,
With you right behind me, my suffering

Con tu sarcasmo mi dolor. Ahora silencio,
Por si alguno pretende que me quejo: es más digno
Sentirse vivo en medio de la angustia
Que ignorar con los grandes de este mundo,
Cerrados en su limbo tras las puertas de oro.

D: Después de todo, ¿quién dice que no sea
Tu Dios, no tu demonio, el que te habla?
Amigo ya no tienes sino es éste
Que te incita y despierta, padeciendo contigo.
Mas mira cómo el alba a la ventana
Te convoca a vivir sin ganas otro día.
Pues el mundo no aprueba al desdichado,
Recuerda la sonrisa y, como aquel que aguarda,
Álzate y vé, aunque aquí nada esperes.

Made worse by your sarcasm. But enough already,
Lest anyone should think I'm complaining: better
To feel the anguish of being alive
Than know nothing, like the ones who run the world,
Locked in their void behind golden doors.

D: In the end, who can say it's not
Your demon but God who's talking to you?
You know that I'm the only friend you've got
To shake you up a little, and suffer with you.
But look at the way the sunrise in the window
Calls you to live another pointless day.
The world does not approve of the unhappy, so
Remember to smile and, like the one watching over you,
Rise and shine, though here you can hope for nothing.

RÍO VESPERTINO

Dejando atrás el claustro, donde suenan
Ecos de voces nuevas y nonatas,
Por la vereda del molino viejo
Se llega al río, en cuya margen hay
Edificios de ámbar ceniciento,
Barcas ociosas que el verano esperan
Por la corriente estrecha, entre los juncos
Y estos olmos de hermosura increíble.
Está todo abstraído en una pausa
De silencio y quietud. Tan sólo un mirlo
Estremece con el canto la tarde.
Su destino es más puro que el del hombre
Que para el hombre canta, pretendiendo
Ser voz significante de la grey,
La conciencia insistente en esa huida
De las almas. Contemplación, sosiego,
El instante perfecto, que tal fruto
Madura, inútil es para los otros,
Condenando al poeta y su tarea
De ver en unidad el ser disperso,
El mundo fragmentario donde viven.
Sueño no es lo que al poeta ocupa,
Mas la verdad oculta, como el fuego
Subyacente en la tierra. Son los otros,
Traficantes de sueños infecundos,
Quienes despiertan en la muerte un día,
Pobres al fin. ¿De qué le vale al hombre
Ganar su vida mientras pierde el alma,
Si sólo un pensamiento vale el mundo?
Desatendido queda por los otros
El sentido profundo del trabajo
Que ocupó con amor a tantas vidas,
No que el amor así perdido busque

Evening River

Leaving the cloister behind, and its echoes
Of voices new and unborn,
You follow the old mill path down
To the river, the buildings along its banks
Glowing a grayish amber,
Idle boats waiting for summer
Along the narrow current through the reeds
And these gorgeous elms.
Everything is abstracted in a pause
Of silent stillness. Just one blackbird
Sends ripples through the afternoon with his song.
His destiny is purer than a man's
Who sings for people, trying
To be the voice in the crowd that means something,
The steady conscience of these souls
In flight. Tranquility, contemplation,
The instant perfect as a ripe
Fruit, are useless to everyone else,
And this condemns the poet and his task
Of seeing the unity in scattered being,
The shattered world they live in.
Poets don't deal in dreams
But in hidden truth, like fire
Burning in layers under the earth. It's the others,
Traffickers in sterile dreams,
Who wake up dead one day,
Poor in the end. What good does it do
To earn a living and lose your soul
If a single thought is worth as much as the world?
The profound sense of the work
That so many lives have taken up with love
Isn't even noticed by the others,
Not that such love, lost, is looking

Elogio corruptor, honor innoble,
Pero amor en amor quiere moneda,
Aunque sólo en amar halla su precio.
Alguno en tiempos idos se acogía
Al muro propio, al libro y al amigo,
Mas ahora vería roto el muro,
Vacío el libro y el amigo inútil.
Aquéllos son los más, tienen la tierra
Y apenas si un rincón queda asignado
Para el poeta, como muerto en vida.
Es la patria madrastra avariciosa,
Exigiendo el sudor, la sangre, el semen
A cambio del olvido y del destierro.
No importa la existencia, el tiempo dado
Para justificarla, así se muere
No de una muerte actual sino futura.
El alma, adoctrinada en hecatombes,
Del gobierno de Dios ya descreída,
Político eficaz cree al demonio.
Verdad es vehemencia de la masa,
Gloria es complicidad en algo impuro;
Ajado en toda cosa está el encanto,
El fruto deseado amarga ahora
Y un círculo de sombra encierra al día.
Con tácita premura en cada ciclo
La primavera acerca más la muerte
Y adondequiera que los ojos miren
Memoria de la muerte sólo encuentran.
Pero desesperada la esperanza
Insiste al revivir la savia nueva,
Con frágil insistencia, como en marzo
La campanilla blanca rompe el suelo
Desolado por el cierzo y la escarcha.
¿Es del suelo la flor, o acaso al aire
Debe forma, color, gracia y aroma?
Sin raíz, es mejor. La tierra pide

For praise or tainted honors;
Love's only currency is love,
Though only in loving does it learn its cost.
Long ago a person could take refuge
In his own walls, in a book and in a friend,
But now you would find the walls broken,
The book empty and the friend feckless.
The others are everywhere, they own the earth
And they scarcely leave even a little corner
For the poet, who lives as if posthumously.
His country is nothing but a greedy stepmother
Demanding sweat, blood and semen
In exchange for exile and oblivion.
Existence doesn't count, nor the time
Given to justify it, and so you die
Not of a death right now but in the future.
The soul has been conditioned in catastrophes,
Governed by a God that's been discredited,
The devil having taken over politics.
The fury of the crowd is the only truth,
Fame is complicity in something corrupt;
Enchantment is disdained in any case,
The fruit that you desired is bitter now
And a circle of darkness is closing over the day.
Springtime brings death closer
A little faster with every cycle
And everywhere you look
Reminders of death are all you see.
Yet even in the midst of such despair
Hope insists on reviving the new sap,
With delicate persistence as in March
When the hard ground ravaged by frost and wind
Is broken by the little white bellflower.
Does the flower come out of the earth, or perhaps it owes
Its form and color and grace and scent to the air?
Better to have no roots. The earth

Demasiado, y el aire es generoso
Hacia las criaturas de este suelo,
Cuando el camino de la luz procura
Su oscura fe. Aquella cosa importa
De cuya fe conocimiento viene,
Piedra angular de las generaciones
Que labraron con fe lo no creído,
Seguros, no en las cosas que veían,
Pues fe no necesita lo visible;
Fe, contra toda razón, es algo ciego,
Sombra del pensamiento aquietadora.
Si la voz del poeta no es oída,
¿Sino mejor no es para el poeta?
Del hombre aprende el hombre la palabra,
Mas el silencio sólo en Dios lo aprende.
En la paz vespertina, más humilde
Que el júbilo animal a la mañana,
Lo renunciado es poseído ahora,
Cuando la luz su espada ya depuso
En el tiempo sin tiempo, consumando
La identidad del día y de la noche.
El viento fantasmal entre los olmos
Las hojas idas mueve y las futuras.
Está dormido el mirlo. Las estrellas
No descienden al agua todavía.

Demands too much, and air is generous
With the creatures of this dirt,
When the path of light negotiates
Its faith in the dark. And that's a question
Of whose faith can know anything,
Jagged stone of the generations
Who faithfully tried to shape what they didn't believe,
Certain, but not of what they could see,
Since faith has no need for the visible;
Faith, against all reason, is something blind,
The shadow of a thought that's comforting.
If the poet's voice is never heard,
Isn't that all the better for the poet?
People learn to talk from one another,
But silence is learned from God alone.
In the peace of early evening, more humble
Than the animal joy of morning,
Whatever you've renounced is now possessed,
When light has sheathed its sword
In timeless time, consummating
The union of day and night.
The ghostly breeze in the elms
Stirs the leaves long gone and the ones to come.
The blackbird is asleep. The stars
Have not yet dipped into the river.

from

Vivir Sin Estar Viviendo

To Live Without Being Alive

[1944–1949]

EL ÁRBOL

Al lado de las aguas está, como leyenda,
En su jardín murado y silencioso,
El árbol bello dos veces centenario,
Las poderosas ramas extendidas,
Cerco de tanta hierba, entrelazando hojas,
Dosel donde una sombra edénica subsiste.

Bajo este cielo nórdico nacido,
Cuya luz es tan breve, e incierta aun siendo breve,
Apenas embeleso estival lo traspasa y exalta
Como a su hermano el plátano del mediodía,
Sonoro de cigarras, junto del cual es grato
Dejar morir el tiempo divinamente inútil.

Tras el invierno horrible, cuando sólo la llama
Conforta aquella espera del revivir futuro,
Al pie del árbol brotan lágrimas de la nieve,
Corolas de azafrán, jacintos, asfódelos,
Con pujanza vernal de la tierra, y fielmente
De nueva juventud el árbol se corona.

Son entonces los días, algunos despejados,
Algunos nebulosos, más tibios de este clima,
Sueño septentrional que el sol casi no rompe,
Y hacia el estanque vienen rondas de mozos rubios:
Temblando, tantos cuerpos ligeros, queda el agua;
Vibrando, tantas voces timbradas, queda el aire.

Entre sus mocedades, vida prometedora,
Aunque pronto marchita en usos tristes,
Raro es aquel que siente, a solas algún día

The Tree

It stands beside the water, like a legend,
Within its walled and silent garden,
The beautiful tree two centuries old,
Its powerful branches reaching in all directions,
Surrounded by so much grass, its leaves interlaced,
Canopy casting an Edenic shade.

Born underneath this northern sky,
Whose light is so brief, and equally uncertain,
A summery spell scarcely stirs or exalts it
As it does its brother plane tree at midday
With the sounds of crickets, near which it feels good
To let time die a divinely useless death.

After the horrible winter, when only a warm fire
Could comfort that hope for future renewal,
At the foot of the tree the snow's bright tears break out,
Corollas of saffron, hyacinths, asphodels,
With the vernal force of the earth, and faithfully
The tree is crowned again with fresh new youth.

Then come the days, some clear,
Some cloudy, warmer than usual here,
A northern slumber all but unbroken by sun,
And toward the pond come bands of blond young men:
The water trembling with so many light bodies;
The air vibrating with so many ringing voices.

Among these youths, and life with all its promise,
Though soon to be withered with sad misuse,
One strange boy touches the trunk one day

En hora apasionada, la mano sobre el tronco,
La secreta premura de la savia, ascendiendo
Tal si fuera el latido de su propio destino.

Cuando la juventud el mundo es ancho,
Su medida tan vasta como vasto el deseo,
La soledad ligera, placentero ese irse,
Mirando sin nostalgia cosas y criaturas
Amigas un momento, en blanco la memoria
De recuerdos, que un día serán fardo cansado.

Atrás quedan los otros, repitiendo
Sin urgencia interior los gestos aprendidos,
Legitimados siempre por un provecho estéril;
Ya grey apareada, de hijos productora,
Pasiva ante el dolor como bestia asombrada,
Viva en un limbo idéntico al que en la muerte encuentra.

Pero ocurre una pausa en medio del camino;
La mirada que anhela, vuelta hacia lo futuro,
Es nostálgica ahora, vuelta hacia lo pasado;
Una fatiga nueva, alerta ya a esos ecos
De voces que se fueron, suspensas en el aire
Las preguntas de siempre, por nadie respondidas.

Y el mozo iluso es viejo, él mismo ignora cómo
Entre sueños fue el tiempo malgastado;
Ya su faz reflejada extraña le aparece,
Más que su faz extraña su conciencia,
De donde huyó el fervor trocado por disgusto,
Tal pájaro extranjero en nido que otro hizo.

Mientras, en su jardín, el árbol bello existe
Libre del engaño mortal que al tiempo engendra,
Y si la luz escapa de su cima a la tarde,

And feels, for a passionate moment,
The secret surge of its rising sap
As if it were the pulse of his own destiny.

When you're young and the world feels wide,
Its scope as vast as desire itself,
And solitude light, it's pleasant to set out,
Free of nostalgia, seeing all living things
As friends for a moment, the mind clear, empty
Of memories, which later will be a heavy burden to bear.

He leaves the others behind, repeating
The hollow gestures they've all learned,
Legitimate always by virtue of a sterile utility;
Paired up out of the crowd, producing children,
Passive before their pain like frightened animals,
Alive in a limbo that's the same as death.

But halfway down the road he has to pause;
The gaze of desire, turned toward the future,
Is now nostalgic, turned toward the past;
And he feels a fresh fatigue, alert now to those echoes
Of voices gone, suspended in the air
Like eternal questions no one ever answers.

And the deluded youth is old, not knowing himself
How the time between dreams was so ill spent;
And his face seen in reflection appears strange,
More than his face his consciousness feels strange,
From which the passion fled, traded for discontent,
Like a foreign bird in a nest built by another.

Meanwhile, in its garden, the gorgeous tree exists
Free of the mortal deceptions wrought by time,
And if light abandons its crown in late afternoon

Cuando aquel aire ganan lentamente las sombras,
Sólo aparece triste a quien triste le mira:
Ser de un mundo perfecto donde el hombre es extraño.

As shadows are slowly taking over the air,
It looks sad only to the sad observer:
Creation of a perfect world where man is a stranger.

EL PRISIONERO

Atrás quedan los muros
Y las rejas, respira
La libertad ahora,
A solas con tu vida.

Como nube en el aire,
Como luz en el alba,
Mira la tierra toda
Abierta ante tu planta.

Mas libertad sin nadie
Ganaste, y te parece

Victoria desolada,
Figura de la muerte.

The Prisoner

The walls, the bars
Behind you, now
You can breathe freedom,
All alone with your life.

Like a cloud in the sky,
Like light at sunrise,
See how the whole world
Opens before your stride.

But what you've won
Is freedom with no one,

A desolate victory,
A form of death.

EL NOMBRE

Llegue quedo tu paso
Sobre la tierra, adonde
Brilla con sombra roja
Esa haya, y vecino
Con su sombra de oro
Ese castaño, al toque
De la luz misma. Pasa
Esta hora contigo
A solas, tal si fuese
Una hora postrera,
Una primera, acaso
Umbral de muerte o vida,
Mientras gira la tarde
De indecible sosiego
Y hermosura indecible.
Con su cielo está el mundo;
Bien nuevas son las hojas;
Las flores del manzano,
Nieve mejor, sin viento
Profusamente caen;
La hierba sueño ofrece
Para el amor, y el aire
Respirado es delicia.
Hasta parece el hombre,
Tú quieto, entre los otros,
Un árbol más, amigo
Al fin en paz, la sola
Paz de toda la tierra.
Recoge el alma, y mira;
Pocos miran el mundo.
La realidad por nadie
Vista, paciente espera,
Tal criatura joven,

The Name

You set foot softly
On this ground where
The red shade of that
Beech tree shines, and close by
With its golden shade
That chestnut, touched
By sunlight. This hour
Goes by with you
Alone, as if it were
The final hour,
Or the first, perhaps
The doorway of death or life,
While the unspeakably
Calm and unspeakably
Lovely afternoon spins.
The world is with its sky;
The leaves are budding green;
The apple blossoms,
More like snow, windlessly
Fall in profusion;
The grass offers a dream
Of love, and the air
You breathe is delicious.
Even a man, you held still,
Seems to be one more
Tree among the others, a friend
Finally at peace, the only
Peace on the planet.
Gather your soul, and look;
So few look at the world.
The reality no one sees
Waits patiently,
Like someone young

Espejo en unos ojos
Enamorados. Calla.
En este instante todo
Gesto humano resulta
Ocioso, y sólo un nombre
Pensado, mas no dicho
(Abril, abril), perfecto
Lo contiene y da forma
Única suficiente.

Reflecting the love
In your eyes. Quiet now.
In this moment any
Movement you make is
Leisurely, and just one name
In thought but unspoken
(April, April) contains it
Perfectly and gives it
Its one true form.

LA FECHA

También en cielo extraño
Y en extraña comarca,
Cuando al primer otoño
Dice un pájaro el alba.

En el umbral hortensias
Con cielo claro, luego
El mar sin la memoria
Todo, al abrir de un sueño.

Allá están los caminos,
A esta luz todavía
Vacíos, y entre ellos
Uno aguarda tu ida.

No preguntes si vale
La pena haber venido,
Sino déjate, piensa
Que un dios es hoy tu amigo.

A Day

Under a foreign sky
And in a foreign place,
When at the start of autumn
A bird announces dawn.

Hydrangeas at the doorstep,
A clear sky, then the sea,
All swept free of memory,
Opening on a dream.

Out there all the roads,
Still empty in this light,
And one of them is the one
Certain to take you away.

Don't ask what it was worth
For you to have gotten here,
Just let it be, and think
Some god is your friend today.

EL VIENTO Y EL ALMA

Con tal vehemencia el viento
Viene del mar, que sus sones
Elementales contagian
El silencio de la noche.

Solo en tu cama le escuchas
Insistente en los cristales
Tocar, llorando y llamando
Como perdido sin nadie.

Mas no es él quien en desvelo
Te tiene, sino otra fuerza
De que tu cuerpo es hoy cárcel,
Fue viento libre, y recuerda.

The Wind and the Soul

The wind blows in off the ocean
So furiously its elemental sounds
Spread their dark contagion
All through the night's silence.

Alone in your bed you hear it
Hammering at the windows,
Crying and calling out
Like someone lost, alone.

It's not that homeless soul
Who troubles you, but another force
Imprisoned in your body
Was once free as that wind

And it remembers.

EL SINO

El alma en armonía, a solas
Quiere vivir junto a lo amado,
Con el silencio que una rosa
  Se entreabre en su ramo.

El alma en desacuerdo, a solas
Debe morir junto a lo extraño,
Con el silencio que una rosa
  Se deshoja en su ramo.

Destiny

The soul in harmony
Wants to be near its love
As silently as a rose
   Opening on a branch.

The soul that's out of tune
Must die alone estranged
As silently as a rose
   Letting its petals fall.

OTRAS RUINAS

La torre que con máquinas ellos edificaron,
Por obra de las máquinas conoce la ruina,
Tras de su ordenación quedando a descubierto
Fuerzas instigadoras de torpes invenciones:
La carencia que nunca pudo esperar hartura,
La saciedad que nunca quiso guardar templanza;
Como dos enemigos frente a frente,
Hambre y frío de una parte, soberbia y avaricia de la otra.

La ruina ha clamado por suyos tantos muros
Sobre huecos disformes bostezando, ayer morada
De la cual sin cobijo subsiste irónico detalle:
Chimenea manchada por humo de las noches
Idas, como los cuerpos allá templados en invierno,
O tramo de escalera que conduce a la nada
Donde sus moradores irrumpieron con gesto estupefacto,
En juego del azar, sin coherencia de destino.

Intacto nada queda, aunque parezca
Firme, como esas otras casas hoy vacías,
Hacia cuyos salones las ventanas permiten
El vislumbre de espejos, oros sobrecargados,
Entre los cuales discurría la vanidad solemne
De ilustres aristócratas, eminentes políticos, acaudalados
 financieros,
Que al hablar despertaban un eco de murmullos complacidos
Y el respeto debido al rango y la fortuna.

El recinto donde las damas, dispensando
Una taza de te, medían su sonrisa según el visitante,
Bajo de cuyos techos festejaron múltiples las bujías
Íntimas reuniones y brillantes saraos, o en ocasión más rara
El matrimonio ventajoso por dos familias esperado,

Other Ruins

The towers built by machines,
Machines knocked down,
Aggressive powers with crude inventions
Following orders to be known by all:
The emptiness that could never hope to be filled,
The fullness that could never be contained;
Like two enemies face to face,
Hunger and cold on one side, arrogance and greed on the other.

Ruin has claimed for its own so many walls
Above misshapen yawning holes in the ground,
Some ironic remnant all that's left of what was a home:
Part of a chimney stained with smoke from nights
Gone by, like the bodies warmed by its fire in winter,
Or a flight of stairs climbing into nothing
Where the residents rush in with an astonished look,
Playthings of chance, which makes no sense.

Nothing is left intact, even what seems
Solid, like those other now vacant houses
Whose drawing room windows reveal
A glimpse of mirrors encrusted with gold
Where illustrious aristocrats, eminent politicians, wealthy
financiers
Once held forth with solemn vanity
And when they spoke were echoed by assuring murmurs
And all respect due to their class and wealth.

The corner where ladies serving tea
Measured their smiles to suit the visitor,
Under whose roofs so many candelabras glimmered
Amid intimate gatherings and brilliant salons,
Or occasionally a wedding to both families' advantage,

Ya se encuentra desnudo y alberga solamente
La sede de socorros, a cuyas oficinas
Supervivientes fantasmales llegan.

La discreción reticente de estas calles,
Rumbo a las alamedas de algún parque, todas
En perspectiva acorde con el cielo moroso,
Hechas para los pasos de ocioso transeúnte,
El matinal jinete o la nocturna carretela,
Ve su color de perla por hollín mancillado,
Ofendido a diario su sosiego entre las sacudidas
Vulgares de la vida que aún subsiste.

Como desierto, adonde muchedumbres
Marchan dejando atrás la ruta decisiva,
Estéril era esta ciudad. Aquélla
Que con saber sin fe quiso mover montañas;
Toda ella monstruosa masa insuficiente:
Su alimento los frutos de colonias distantes,
Su prisa lucha inútil con espacio y con tiempo,
Su estruendo limbo ensordecedor de la conciencia.

El hombre y la ciudad se corresponden
Como al durmiente el sueño, al pecador la trasgresión oculta;
Ella y él recusaron al silencio de las cosas
Hasta el refugio último: el aire inviolado,
De donde aves maléficas precipitaron muerte
Sobre la grey culpable, hacinada, indefensa,
Pues quien vivir a solas ya no sabe, morir a solas ya no debe.
Del dios al hombre es don postrero la ruina.

Is now reduced to nothing more
Than a first aid station
Where ghostly survivors gather.

The reserved discretion of these streets
Leading toward the trees of some park, everything
Laid out just so under the grim sky,
Designed as paths for leisurely strollers,
The morning horseman or evening carriage,
Sees their pearly color smeared with soot,
Their calm disturbed every day by the vulgar
Shakings of whatever life persists.

Like a desert where swarms of people
Wander aimlessly, this city
Was barren. It tried
To move mountains with skill but no faith,
And all that monstrous power was not enough:
Its food the fruits of distant colonies,
Its bustle a useless fight against space and time,
Its thunderous noise enough to deafen consciousness.

Man and the city are linked
Like dreams and the sleeper, like the sinner and the secret vice;
Now they are pulled back into the silence of things,
Back to the final refuge: the inviolate air
From which malevolent birds poured down death
On the stacked up, defenseless, guilty masses,
Since whoever doesn't know how to live alone shouldn't die
alone.
Ruins are the gods' last gift to man.

EL POETA

La edad tienes ahora que él entonces,
Cuando en el tiempo de la siembra y la danza,
Hijos de anhelo moceril que se despierta,
Tu sueño, tu esperanza, tu secreto,
Aquellos versos fueron a sus manos
Para mostrar y hallar signo de vida.

Mucho nos dicen, desde el pasado, voces
Ilustres, ascendientes de la palabra nuestra,
Y las de lengua extraña, cuyo acento
Experiencia distinta nos revela. Mas las cosas,
El fuego, el mar, los árboles, los astros,
Nuevas siempre aparecen.

Nuevas y arcanas, hasta que al fin traslucen
Un día en la expresión de aquel poeta
Vivo de nuestra lengua, en el contemporáneo
Que infunde por nosotros,
Con su obra, la fe, la certidumbre
Maga de nuestro mundo visible e invisible.

Con reverencia y con amor así aprendiste,
Aunque en torno los hombres no curen de la imagen
Misteriosa y divina de las cosas,
De él, a mirar quieto, como
Espejo, sin el cual la creación sería
Ciega, hasta hallar su mirada en el poeta.

Aquel tiempo pasó, o tú pasaste,
Agitando una estela temporal ilusoria,
Adonde estaba él, cuando tenía

The Poet

You're now the same age as he was then,
When in the dance of seed time,
Boys whose desire was just awakening,
Your dream, your hope, your secret,
Those poems of his were given to you
To show you how life could be.

Out of the past they say so much, these voices
That make our language glow and soar,
And ones in other languages, whose accent
Shows us different kinds of experience. But things,
Fire, ocean, trees, stars,
Always appear new.

New and hidden until finally they shine
One day in the language of that living
Poet of ours,
Who infuses us,
Through his work, with faith, with magical
Certainty in our world, seen and unseen.

And so, though men around you may not be healed
By the divine mysterious image of things,
You learned, lovingly, reverently,
From him, to be still and to look, like
A mirror, without which creation would be
Blind until finding its sight in the poet's gaze.

That moment passed, or you did,
Leaving an illusory wake in time,
Where he was when

La misma edad que hoy tienes:
Lo que su fe sabía y la tuya buscaba,
Ahora has encontrado.

Agradécelo pues, que una palabra
Amiga mucho vale
En nuestra soledad, en nuestro breve espacio
De vivos, y nadie sino tú puede decirle,
A aquel que te enseñara adónde y cómo crece:
Gracias por la rosa del mundo.

Para el poeta hallarla es lo bastante,
E inútil el renombre u olvido de su obra,
Cuando en ella un momento se unifican,
Tal uno son amante, amor y amado,
Los tres complementarios luego y antes dispersos:
El deseo, la rosa y la mirada.

He was the same age you are now:
What his faith knew and yours was looking for,
Now you've found.

So thank him, since a friendly
Word is worth so much
In our solitude, in our moment
Among the living, and no one but you can tell him,
The one who taught you where and how to grow:
Thank you for the world that is a rose.

For a poet that discovery is enough,
And the fame or forgetting of his work doesn't matter,
When in that rose the lover,
Love and the beloved come together,
Made one where before they were separate:
Desire, the rose and the gaze.

UN CONTEMPORÁNEO

Le conocí hace ya tanto tiempo:
Déjeme que recuerde. Si la memoria falla
A mi edad, cuando trata de imaginarse algo
Que en años mozos fuimos, aún más cuando persigue
La figura del hombre sólo visto un momento.

Nunca pensé que alguien viniera a preguntarme
Por tal persona, sin familiar, amigo,
Posición o fortuna; viviendo oscuramente,
Con los gestos diarios de cualquiera
A quien ya nadie nombra tras de muerto.

Que de espejo nos sirva
El prójimo, y nuestra propia imagen
Observemos en él, mas no la suya,
Ocurre a veces. Quien interroga a otros
Por un desconocido, debe contentarse
Con lo que halla, aun cuando sea huella
Ajena superpuesta a la que busca.

Era de edad mediana
Al conocerlo yo, enseñando,
No sé, idioma o metafísica, en puesto subalterno,
Como extraño que ha de ganar la vida
Por malas circunstancias y carece de apoyo.

A esta ciudad había venido
Desde el norte, donde antes estuvo
En circunstancias aún peores; ya conoce
Aquella gente práctica y tacaña, que buscando
Va por la vida sólo rendimiento,
Y poco rendimiento de tal hombre traslucía.

A Contemporary

I knew him quite some time ago;
Let me remember. If at my age
Memory fails when it tries to imagine something
We were when young, it's even worse when it attempts to track
The figure of someone known for just a moment.

I never thought anyone would ask me
About such a person, with no family, friend,
Position or fortune; living unnoticed,
With the routine gestures of anyone
Nobody ever mentions once they're dead.

It happens sometimes
That our neighbor may serve
As our mirror, and in him we see
Our own image more than his. Whoever asks others
About someone unknown has to be satisfied
With what he finds, even if it's just a faint trace
Superimposed on what he's looking for.

He was middle aged
When I met him, teaching,
I don't know what, language or metaphysics, in a lowly job,
Like a stranger who's had to make his way
Through bad luck and with no other means of support.

He had come to this city
From the north, where he had been
Even worse off, among
Those stingy, pragmatic people who seek
In life nothing but production,
And such a man had little production to show.

Aquí se hallaba a gusto, en lo posible
Para quien no parecía a gusto en parte alguna,
Aun cuando, ido, no quisiera
Regresar, ni a varios conocidos
Locales recordó. Así trataba acaso
Que lo pasado fuera pasado realmente
Y comenzar en limpio nueva etapa.

No le vi mucho, rehusando,
A lo que entiendo, el trato y compañía,
Acaso huraño y receloso en algo
Para mí indiferente. Poco hablaba,
Aunque en rara ocasión hablaba todo
Lo callado hasta entonces, entero, abrupto,
Y pareciendo luego avergonzado.

Pero seamos francos: yo no le quería
Bien, y un día, conversando
Temas insustanciales, el tiempo, los deportes,
La política, sentí temor extraño
Que en burla, no hacia mí, sino a los hombres todos
En mí representados, fuera a sacar la lengua.

Lo que pensó, amó odió, le dejó indiferente,
Ignoro; como lo ignoro igual hasta de otros
Que conocí mejor. Nuestro vivir, de muchedumbre
A solas con un dios, un demonio o una nada,
Supongo que era el suyo también. ¿Por qué no habría de serlo?

Su pensamiento hoy puede leerse
Tras la obra, y ella sabrá decirle
Más que yo. Aunque supongo
Tales escritos sin valor alguno,
Y aquí ninguno se cuidaba de su autor o ellos.

He was comfortable here, as much as anyone could be
Who seemed uncomfortable anywhere,
Though once he'd gone he never tried
To return, not even to revisit
The places he knew. Maybe that's how he dealt
With the fact that the past was truly past
And he was starting again with a clean slate.

I never saw much of him; from what I could tell,
He didn't care for other people's company,
Perhaps he was some kind of hermit, afraid of something
That didn't interest me. He scarcely spoke,
Though when he did he said everything
Bottled up until then, and all at once, in a rush,
And afterward seemed ashamed.

But let's be honest: I didn't like him
Much, and one day, exchanging
Small talk, weather, sports,
Politics, I felt a strange fear
When he jokingly stuck out his tongue, not at me but at people
In general, of whom I was merely a representative.

Whatever he thought, loved, hated, what left him cold,
I have no idea; the same as I hardly knew such things
About people I knew better. Our way of living, alone in crowds
With a god, a devil or nothing at all,
Was also his, I suppose. Why wouldn't it be?

His thought can now be read
In his published work, and it can tell you
More than I ever could. Though I suppose
Such writings are of negligible worth
And nobody cares anymore about them or their author.

Esta fama postrera no la mueve,
En mozos tan despiertos, amor de hacer justicia,
Sino gusto de hallar razón contra nosotros
Los viejos, el estorbo palmario en el camino,
Al cual no basta el apartar, mas el desprecio
Debe añadirse. Pues, ¿acaso
Vive desconocido el poeta futuro?

Sabemos que un poeta es otra cosa;
La chispa que le anima pronto prende
En quienes junto a él cruzan la vida,
Sus versos aceptados tal moneda corriente.
Lope fue siempre el listo Lope, vivo o muerto.

Tan vulgar como quiera será el vulgo,
Pero la voz del vulgo es voz divina,
Por estos tiempos nuestros a lo menos;
Y el vulgo era ignorante de ese hombre
Mientras viviera, en signo
Que siempre ignorará su póstuma excelencia.

La sociedad es justa, a todos trata
Como merecen; si hay exceso
Primero, con idéntico exceso retrocede,
Recobrando nivel. Piense de alguno,
Festejado tal dios por muchedumbres,
Por esas muchedumbres tal animal colgado.
Bien que ello nos repugne, justicia pura y simple.

Mas eso no se aplica a nuestro hombre.
¿Acaso hubo exceso en el olvido
Que vivió día a día? Hecho a medida
Del propio ser oscuro, exacto era; y a la muerte

Fame after the fact, for boys like us,
Just starting out, was not a matter of justice
But of figuring out why the old men
Were set against us, a blatant obstacle in our path,
Which it wasn't enough to avoid, but on top of that
We had to add disrespect. So maybe
Some future poet goes unrecognized?

We know that a poet is something else;
The spark that drives him soon ignites
Whoever crosses his path,
His lines are taken as currency.
Lope was always clever Lope, alive or dead.

The masses are always going to be vulgar,
But the voice of the masses is the voice of God,
At least in times like these;
And the masses knew nothing of this man
When he was alive, a sure sign
They'll never know of any future excellence.

Society is fair, it treats everyone
As they deserve; if at first it gives
Too much, then it takes it away,
Balancing the scales. Think of someone
Adored as a god by admiring crowds,
And by the same crowds strung up like an animal.
As little as we may like it, it's justice pure and simple.

But this does not apply to our good man.
Perhaps he was too much forgotten
In the way he lived day to day? Measured
To the size of his own obscurity, oblivion fit; and in death

Se lleva aquello que tomamos
De la vida, o lo que ella nos da: olvido
Acá, y olvido allá para él. Es lo mismo.

Whatever we took from life, or what it gives us,
Is taken away: oblivion here
And oblivion there for him. It's the same thing.

Translator's note: Lope de Vega (1562–1635), one of the masters of the Golden Age, is considered one of Spain's greatest poets and dramatists.

LAS EDADES

Trágicamente extraños, desprendidos
Desde su eternidad, entre los astros
Libres del tiempo, así aparecen hoy
Por los museos. Pálidos fantasmas
En concilio, convocados por el sueño,
Sobre la escalinata polvorienta,
En el dintel de las columnas rotas,
Vuelta irreal tanta hermosura aún viva.

Imaginados por un pueblo remoto,
De su temblor divino forma eran
(Como la rosa es forma del deseo);
Y en el bronce, en el marfil y el mármol,
Presidiendo los actos de la vida,
De terror y de gozo solos dispensadores,
En perfección erguidos, iba a ellos,
Con murmullo confuso, la palabra.

Un pueblo existe por su intuición de lo divino
Y es voz del sino que halla eco en historia,
Movido del ahinco indisoluble
De su tierra y su dios; así creando
Con lo invisible lo visible,
Con el sueño el acto, con el ánimo el gesto,
Del existir dando razón el mito,
Adonde nace, crece, engendra y muere.

Mas un pueblo al morir siente sus dioses
Vulnerables también, lo divino y lo humano
Sin magia ni virtud, de extraños luego presa
Cuanto era de otros el centro y el contorno:
Los trabajos del mar, y la labranza

The Ages

Tragically estranged, cast out
From their eternity amid
The timeless stars, that's how they look
Today in the museums. Pale ghosts
In conference, convened by dreams,
On the dusty staircase,
On the lintel between the broken columns,
So much still living beauty turned unreal.

Imagined by a people far removed,
They were a form of some divine vibration
(Just as the rose is a form of desire);
And in bronze, in ivory and in marble,
Presiding over the events of life,
The sole dispensers of terror and pleasure,
Erect in their perfection, they drew
Words murmured to them in confused worship.

A people exists in its sense of the divine
And is the voice of destiny finding an echo in history,
Moved by the indissoluble bond
Of its land and its god; creating
With the invisible the visible,
With the dream the deed, with the will the gesture,
Existence given meaning only by myth,
Where it is born, grows, propagates and dies.

But a people when it's dying feels its gods
Are vulnerable too, the divine and the human
Bereft of magic, virtue, merely caught
Estranged in the midst of what enveloped others:
The works of the sea, the labor

Del campo, y la paz del caserío;
Lo que unido en los dioses es la vida
Y desunido es apetencia de la muerte.

Ahora, así humillados en un gesto
Ya ineficaz, se sobreviven
Preciosos sin valor, como la concha
Índica, de su perla despojada,
Cuando lejos del abismo nativo
Inerme yace a las injurias,
Sólo presea de un niño o de un enamorado,
Porque el iris cambiante le recuerda unos ojos.

La piedra cariada, el mármol corroído,
Es descomposición del dios, segura
De consumarse bajo el aire, como
Bajo la tierra la del hombre;
Ambos, el dios y el hombre, iguales
Ante el ultraje igual del azar y del tiempo
Cuyo poder los rige, y aceptada
La humildad de perderse en el olvido.

En la penumbra polvorienta pasan hoy
Seres grises; con ojos asombrados
Miran sin ver aquellos cuerpos duros
Orgullosos: el anca, el vientre, el lomo
De animales perfectos; los vestigios
Del dios que fue, que exige serlo siempre;
Y hostiles como extraños ofenden su agonía
Con una admiración incrédula.

Of the fields, the peace of the village;
What brought together by the gods is life,
And taken apart is an appetite for death.

Now, humiliated, their expressions
Helpless, they survive
Precious but worthless, like an empty
Shell stripped of its pearl,
Where far from its native depths
It lies undefended against insult,
Priceless only to a child or a lover
Because its changing shimmer reminds them of eyes.

The pitted stone, the corroded marble,
Is a god decaying, surely being
Consumed by the very air, the same way
A man decomposes underground:
Both god and man are equal
Before the equal violations of time and chance
Whose power rules over them, and they accept
The humiliation of being lost in oblivion.

Today in the dusty dimness these gray beings
Walk past them; with frightened eyes
They look without seeing those bodies hard
With pride: buttocks, bellies, backs
Of perfect animals; vestiges
Of the gods they were, who demand to endure always;
And angry at how these strangers offend their agony
With an admiration devoid of belief.

CARA JOVEN

Ahora quisieras recordarte,
Hablar lo mismo que solías
Antes, de ligero y de breve,
Por amor a esta faz tan niña.

Pero los tiempos ya son otros,
Y tú otro del que creías
Entonces. Sólo tu gozo
Es el de siempre si la miras.

Como lluvia clara, conforta;
Como sueño de amanecida,
Alienta; sugiere posibles
E imposibles, como la vida.

Young Face

Now you'd like to remember
And speak as you used to, before,
However lightly and briefly,
Of that childlike face you adored.

But times have changed,
As you have, from the believer
You were then. To look was your only
Pleasure, the same as always.

Like cleansing rain, it comforts;
Like a dream at dawn,
It inspires; it hints at what's possible
And impossible, just like life.

SER DE SANSUEÑA

Acaso allí estará, cuatro costados
Bañados en los mares, al centro la meseta
Ardiente y andrajosa. Es ella, la madrastra
Original de tantos, como tú, dolidos
De ella y por ella dolientes.

Es la tierra imposible, que a su imagen te hizo
Para de sí arrojarte. En ella el hombre
Que otra cosa no pudo, por error naciendo,
Sucumbe de verdad, y como en pago
Ocasional de otros errores inmortales.

Inalterable, en violento claroscuro,
Mírala, piénsala. Árida tierra, cielo fértil,
Con nieves y resoles, riadas y sequías;
Almendros y chumberas, espartos y naranjos
Crecen en ella, ya desierto, ya oasis.

Junto a la iglesia está la casa llana,
Al lado del palacio está la timba,
El alarido ronco junto a la voz serena,
El amor junto al odio, y la caricia junto
A la puñalada. Allí es extremo todo.

La nobleza plebeya, el populacho noble,
La pueblan; dando terratenientes y toreros,
Curas y caballistas, vagos y visionarios,
Guapos y guerrilleros. Tú compatriota,
Bien que ello te repugne, de su fauna.

Las cosas tienen precio. Lo es del poderío
La corrupción, del amor la no correspondencia;
Y ser de aquella tierra lo pagas con no serlo

Sansueña's Child

I wonder if it's still there, four coasts
Washed by oceans, central plateau
Hot and ragged. It is the original
Stepmother of so many, like you,
Aching for her and on account of her.

It is the impossible land, which made you in its image
Only to cast you out. That's where a man
Who couldn't help himself, born by accident,
Is brought low truly, as if to pay
For other immortal errors.

Look and consider: it is unchanging,
In violent chiaroscuro. Arid land, fertile sky,
Sun glare, snowdrifts, floods and droughts;
Almond groves and prickly pear, esparto and oranges
Grow there, now an oasis, now a desert.

Next to a soaring church is a simple house,
Alongside the palace is the card room,
The rough shout alongside the soothing voice,
Love beside hate, and the caress so close
To the stab. Everything taken to extremes.

The plebian nobility, the noble masses,
Cover her; with landlords and bullfighters,
Priests and cowboys, wanderers and visionaries,
Playboys and warriors. You too, countryman,
Much as she repels you, are one of hers.

Everything has its price. The cost of power
Is corruption; of love, to be unrequited;
And to be from that land you pay by not being

De ninguna: deambular, vacuo y nulo,
Por el mundo, que a Sansueña y sus hijos desconoce.

Si en otro tiempo hubiera sido nuestra,
Cuando gentes extrañas la temían y odiaban,
Y mucho era ser de ella; cuando toda
Su sinrazón congénita, y locura hoy,
Como admirable paradoja se imponía.

Vivieron muerte, sí, pero con gloria
Monstruosa. Hoy la vida morimos
En ajeno rincón. Y mientras tanto
Los gusanos, de ella y su ruina irreparable,
Crecen, prosperan.

Vivir para ver esto.
Vivir para ser esto.

From anywhere: to wander nullified
Through the world, which knows nothing of Sansueña and its
children.

In some other time she might have been ours,
When foreign peoples feared and hated her,
And it meant something to have come from her; when all
Her inborn unreason, now gone mad,
Imposed itself as admirable paradox.

They lived death, it's true, but with a monstrous
Glory. Now we're dying living
So far from her. And all the while
The worms, born of her and her irreparable ruin,
Thrive and prosper.

Having to see this.
Having to be this.

Translator's note: Sansueña is the poet's mythical name for his native Spain. It suggests both "without" and "dream" (*sin sueño*), or sleeplessness, in Spanish.

PARA ESTAR CONTIGO

Sé que a solas, aburrido
De estar vivo y quedar muerto,
Pasas el tiempo, o te pasa
El tiempo sin tú quererlo.

Pues el fuego no la anima
Sino en lumbre pasajera,
Entiende la paradoja
De tu existencia incompleta.

La luna a veces es clara,
El aire a veces es tibio,
El cuerpo joven tan puro
Como siempre, y tan perdido.

El sino te lleva, y puedes,
Si así lo quieres, pararle,
Cuando seguir cansa. Entonces
Eres dueño en lo que vale.

Luego la vejez alcanza,
Y con ella ese recelo
De una falla, ajena o tuya,
En el ciclo ya completo.

No digas que no esperabas
Todo ello en el principio,
Y acepta, como si iguales,
Lo esperado y lo vivido.

To Be with You

I know that, alone and tired
Of being both dead and alive,
You pass the time, or it passes you
Whether you like it or not.

Since fire lights up nothing
More than some passing glow,
It grasps the paradox
Of your incomplete existence.

Sometimes the moon is bright,
Sometimes the air is warm,
And the young body is as pure
As ever, and as lost.

Fate leads you, but you can,
Whenever you wish to, stop it,
If following wears you out. And so
You are the master of what matters.

Then old age overtakes you,
And with it that suspicion
Of a flaw, yours or another's,
In the cycle now complete.

Don't say you didn't expect
All this from the beginning,
And accept, as if they were equal,
Your hopes and what you've lived.

LAS ISLAS

Recuerdo que tocamos puerto tras larga travesía,
Y dejando el navío y el muelle, por callejas
(Entre el polvo mezclados pétalos y escamas),
Llegué a la plaza, donde estaban los bazares.
Era grande el calor, la sombra poca.

Con el pecho desnudo iba, distraído
Como si familiares fuesen la villa y sus costumbres,
Y miré en un portal al mercader de sedas
Que desplegaba una, color de aurora, fría a los ojos,
Sintiendo sin tocarla la suavidad escurridiza.

Ante un ciego cantor estuve largo espacio,
Único espectador, y parecía cantar para mí solo.
Compré luego a una niña un ramo de jazmines
Amarillentos, pero en su olor ajado tuvo alivio
La dejadez extraña que empezaba a aquejarme.

Desanudada la faja en mi cintura,
Unos muchachos que pasaban, reían,
Volviendo la cabeza. Acaso me creyeron
Ebrio. Los ojos de uno de ellos eran
Como la noche, profundos y estrellados.

La humedad de la piel pronto se disipaba
Por el aire ardoroso, a cuyo influjo
Mi pereza crecía. Me detuve indeciso,
Acariciando el cuerpo, sintiendo su tibieza
Lisa, como si acariciara un cuerpo ajeno.

Seguí, por parajes nunca vistos,
Mas presentidos, igual a quien camina
Hacia cita amistosa. Deponía la tarde

The Islands

I recall our reaching port at the end of a lengthy crossing,
And leaving the ship and the dock, along narrow streets
(Fish scales and petals mingling with the dust),
I came to a plaza where the merchants were.
It was extremely hot, without much shade.

I strolled with my shirt off, not paying attention
As if the town and its customs were familiar,
And in a doorway I noticed the silk seller
With a bolt unfolded, the color of dawn, cold to the eyes,
And could feel without even touching its slippery smoothness.

I stood for a while in front of a blind singer,
His only audience, and it seemed he was singing for me alone.
Then from a girl I bought a spray of yellow
Jasmine, but it was crumpled and the smell began
To rouse me out of my lethargy.

Some boys passed, turning to laugh
At my naked torso.
Maybe they thought I was drunk.
One of them had eyes as dark
As night, deep and gleaming with stars.

The dampness of my skin suddenly lifted
Into the balmy air, making me feel
Even lazier. I stood there, unsure what to do,
Caressing my body, feeling its smooth
Warmth, as if I were stroking someone else's skin.

I kept on, through places I had never seen,
But had some sense of, like someone walking
To meet a friend. The afternoon was fading

Su fuerza, cuando al fin quise
Buscar reposo ante un umbral cerrado.

Era un barrio tranquilo. Mis párpados pesaban
(Acaso dormí mucho), y al abrirlos de nuevo
Ya el sol estaba bajo en el muro de enfrente.
Una presencia ajena pareció despertarme,
Porque al volver la cara vi una mujer, y sonreía.

Como si de mi anhelo fuese proyección, respuesta
Ante demanda informulada, me miraba, insegura;
Aunque yo nada dije, con gesto silencioso,
Invitándome adentro, me tomó de la mano.
La seguí, con recelo más débil que el deseo.

La sala estaba oscura (ya caía la tarde).
Sobre la estera había almohadas, un cestillo
Anidando manojos de magnolias mojadas,
De excesiva fragancia. Filtró la celosía
Unas palabras de la calle: "Le encontraron muerto".

Las pensé referidas a un camarada,
Quizá presagio de mi sino. Pero ella,
Atrayéndome a sí, sobre la alfombra
El ropaje tiró, como cuchillo sin la vaina,
Fría, dura, flexible, escurridiza.

Mis manos en sus pechos, su cintura
Quebrarse pareció al extenderme sobre ella,
Y en el silencio circundante, al ritmo
De los cuerpos, oí su brazalete,
Queja del ave fabulosa que escapaba.

La oscuridad llenó la sala toda
Cuando saciado y satisfecho quise irme.
En la puerta (ella como mi sombra me seguía),

When finally I tried to find a place
To sit down on a doorstep.

It was a quiet neighborhood. My eyelids drowsed
(Maybe I slept a while), and when I opened them
The sun had set behind the wall across.
A strange presence seemed to wake me,
Because when I looked up I saw a woman, and she was smiling.

As if she were a figment of my longing, the reply
To an unformed question, she looked at me, uncertain;
Though I said nothing, with a wordless gesture
She waved me inside and took my hand.
I followed her, fear weaker than desire.

The room was dark (night had already fallen).
There were pillows on the floor mat, a little basket
Full of damp magnolia blossoms
With a strong scent. Through the shutters
Came voices from the street: "They found him dead."

I thought they were talking about a friend of theirs,
Possibly a forecast of my fate. But pulling me
To her, she threw her clothes on the floor
And she looked like an unsheathed knife,
Cold, hard, sinewy, slippery.

As she pulled me on top, my hands at her breasts,
Her center seemed to split open
And in the room's silence as our bodies moved
I could hear her bracelet,
The cry of a fabulous bird flying away.

It was completely dark by the time
I was spent, and satisfied, I tried to leave.
She followed me like a shadow to the door

Al cruzar su dintel, sentí que entre mis dedos
Quedaba el brazalete, ahora inerte y mudo.

Mucho tiempo ha pasado. No aceptara
Revivir otra vez esta existencia.
Mas no sé qué daría por sólo aquel instante
Revivirlo. Bien sé que apenas tengo con qué tiente
Al destino, ni el destino tentarse dejaría.

Cuando el recuerdo así vuelve sobre sus huellas
(¿No es el recuerdo la impotencia del deseo?),
Es que a él, como a mí, la vejez vence;
Y acaso ya no tengo lo único que tuve:
Deseo, a quien rendida la ocasión le sigue.

And as I crossed the threshold I could feel her bracelet
In my fingers, but it was mute and lifeless.

A lot of time has passed. I wouldn't want
To live my life again.
But I don't know what I'd give to relive just
That moment. I know too well that I have nothing
To tempt fate with and that fate would not even be tempted
anyway.

When memory turns like this to retrace its steps
(Is memory not the impotence of desire?),
It's because age has conquered it, as it has me;
And perhaps I no longer have the one thing I had:
Desire, which chance surrendered to, and followed.

A Note on the Author

Luis Cernuda (1902–1963), one of Spain's most revered and influential modern poets, was born in Seville and came of age in Madrid in the 1930s as a leading member of the cohort of poets and artists known as the Generation of 1927. In 1936 he published the first edition of his collected poems, *La realidad y el deseo (Reality and Desire)*, which was to be expanded and revised twice more over the course of his lifetime. In 1938, in the midst of the Spanish Civil War, he left Spain never to return. He spent nine years teaching in universities in London, Cambridge, and Glasgow before accepting a position at Mount Holyoke College in Massachusetts, migrating to the United States in 1947. He moved to Mexico permanently in 1952, returning briefly to the US in the early 1960s for teaching appointments at San Francisco State College and the University of California at Los Angeles. Previous collections of his poetry in English include *Selected Poems,* translated by Reginald Gibbons (1977); *Written in Water,* collected prose poems, translated by Stephen Kessler (2004, winner of the Lambda Literary Award for gay men's poetry); and *Desolation of the Chimera,* selected later poems, translated by Stephen Kessler (2009, winner of the Harold Morton Landon Translation Award of the Academy of American Poets). He died of a heart attack at age sixty-one in the Mexico City suburb of Coyoacán. This volume is the largest collection of his poetry yet to appear in English.

A Note on the Translator

Stephen Kessler is a poet, prose writer, translator and editor. In addition to his award-winning versions of Luis Cernuda, some of his other translations include *Poems of Consummation* by Vicente Aleixandre, *Save Twilight* by Julio Cortázar, *Heights of Machu Picchu* by Pablo Neruda, and *The Sonnets* by Jorge Luis Borges (as editor and principal translator). His recent books of original writing include *Where Was I?* (prose poems/memoirs), *Need I Say More?* (essays), *Scratch Pegasus* (poems), and *The Mental Traveler* (novel). He lives in Northern California, where from 1999 through 2014 he was founding editor of *The Redwood Coast Review.* For more about Stephen Kessler, visit www.stephenkessler.com.

TITLES FROM BLACK WIDOW PRESS

TRANSLATION SERIES

A Life of Poems, Poems of a Life by Anna de Noailles. Translated by Norman R. Shapiro. Introduction by Catherine Perry.

Approximate Man and Other Writings by Tristan Tzara. Translated and edited by Mary Ann Caws.

Art Poétique by Guillevic. Translated by Maureen Smith.

The Big Game by Benjamin Péret. Translated with an introduction by Marilyn Kallet.

Boris Vian Invents Boris Vian: A Boris Vian Reader. Edited and translated by Julia Older.

Capital of Pain by Paul Eluard. Translated by Mary Ann Caws, Patricia Terry, and Nancy Kline.

Chanson Dada: Selected Poems by Tristan Tzara. Translated with an introduction and essay by Lee Harwood.

Essential Poems and Writings of Joyce Mansour: A Bilingual Anthology. Translated with an introduction by Serge Gavronsky.

Essential Poems and Prose of Jules Laforgue. Translated and edited by Patricia Terry.

Essential Poems and Writings of Robert Desnos: A Bilingual Anthology. Edited with an introduction and essay by Mary Ann Caws.

EyeSeas (Les Ziaux) by Raymond Queneau. Translated with an introduction by Daniela Hurezanu and Stephen Kessler.

Fables in a Modern Key by Pierre Coran. Edited and translated by Norman R. Shapiro. Full-color illustrations by Olga Pastuchiv.

Forbidden Pleasures: New Selected Poems [1924–1949] by Luis Cernuda. Translated by Stephen Kessler.

Furor and Mystery & Other Writings by René Char. Edited and translated by Mary Ann Caws and Nancy Kline.

Guarding the Air: Selected Poems of Gunnar Harding. Translated and edited by Roger Greenwald.

The Inventor of Love & Other Writings by Gherasim Luca. Translated by Julian & Laura Semilian. Introduction by Andrei Codrescu. Essay by Petre Răileanu.

Jules Supervielle: Selected Prose and Poetry. Translated by Nancy Kline and Patricia Terry.

La Fontaine's Bawdy by Jean de La Fontaine. Translated with an introduction by Norman R. Shapiro.

Last Love Poems of Paul Eluard. Translated with an introduction by Marilyn Kallet.

Love, Poetry (L'amour la poésie) by Paul Eluard. Translated with an essay by Stuart Kendall.

Pierre Reverdy: Poems, Early to Late. Translated by Mary Ann Caws and Patricia Terry.

Poems of André Breton: A Bilingual Anthology. Translated with essays by Jean-Pierre Cauvin and Mary Ann Caws.

Poems of A. O. Barnabooth by Valéry Larbaud. Translated by Ron Padgett and Bill Zavatsky.

Poems of Consummation by Vicente Aleixandre. Translated by Stephen Kessler.

Préversities: A Jacques Prévert Sampler. Translated and edited by Norman R. Shapiro.

The Sea and Other Poems by Guillevic. Translated by Patricia Terry. Introduction by Monique Chefdor.

To Speak, to Tell You? Poems by Sabine Sicaud. Translated by Norman R. Shapiro. Introduction and notes by Odile Ayral-Clause.

Forthcoming Translations

Earthlight (Claire de Terre) by André Breton. Translated by Bill Zavatsky and Zack Rogrow. (New and revised edition.)

The Gentle Genius of Cécile Périn: Selected Poems (1906–1956). Edited and translated by Norman R. Shapiro.

MODERN POETRY SERIES

ABC of Translation by Willis Barnstone

An Alchemist with One Eye on Fire by Clayton Eshleman

Anticline by Clayton Eshleman

Archaic Design by Clayton Eshleman

Backscatter: New and Selected Poems by John Olson

Barzakh (Poems 2000–2012) by Pierre Joris

The Caveat Onus by Dave Brinks

City Without People: The Katrina Poems by Niyi Osundare

Concealments and Caprichos by Jerome Rothenberg

Crusader-Woman by Ruxandra Cesereanu. Translated by Adam J. Sorkin. Introduction by Andrei Codrescu.

Curdled Skulls: Poems of Bernard Bador. Translated by the author with Clayton Eshleman.

Endure: Poems by Bei Dao. Translated by Clayton Eshleman and Lucas Klein.

Exile Is My Trade: A Habib Tengour Reader. Translated by Pierre Joris.

Eye of Witness: A Jerome Rothenberg Reader. Edited with commentaries by Heriberto Yepez & Jerome Rothenberg.

Fire Exit by Robert Kelly

Forgiven Submarine by Ruxandra Cesereanu and Andrei Codrescu

from stone this running by Heller Levinson

The Grindstone of Rapport: A Clayton Eshleman Reader

Larynx Galaxy by John Olson

The Love That Moves Me by Marilyn Kallet

Memory Wing by Bill Lavender

Packing Light: New and Selected Poems by Marilyn Kallet

The Present Tense of the World: Poems 2000–2009 by Amina Saïd. Translated with an introduction by Marilyn Hacker.

The Price of Experience by Clayton Eshleman

The Secret Brain: Selected Poems 1995–2012 by Dave Brinks

Signal from Draco: New and Selected Poems by Mebane Robertson

Forthcoming Modern Poetry Titles

An American Unconscious by Mebane Robertson

Essential Poetry (1968–2015) by Clayton Eshleman

Disenchanted City (La Ville desenchantee) by Chantal Bizzini. Edited by Marilyn Kallet and J. Bradford Anderson. Translated by J. Bradford Anderson, Darren Jackson, and Marilyn Kallet.

Funny Way of Staying Alive by Willis Barnstone

The Hexagon by Robert Kelly

Memory by Bernadette Mayer

Soraya (Sonnets) by Anis Shivani

Wrack Lariat by Heller Levinson

LITERARY THEORY / BIOGRAPHY SERIES

Barbaric Vast & Wild: A Gathering of Outside and Subterranean Poetry (Poems for the Millennium, v. 5) Eds: Jerome Rothenberg and John Bloomberg-Rissman

Clayton Eshleman: The Whole Art by Stuart Kendall

Revolution of the Mind: The Life of André Breton by Mark Polizzotti

WWW.BLACKWIDOWPRESS.COM